William Blake

# THE BOOK OF URIZEN

## Introduction by CLARK EMERY
### University of Miami

UNIVERSITY OF MIAMI PRESS
*Coral Gables* • *Florida*

UNIVERSITY OF MIAMI

CRITICAL STUDIES

No. 6

Printed in the United States of America

# Acknowledgments

The text of Blake's poem has been reproduced by permission of the William Blake Trust, from *The Book of Urizen*, published in facsimile edition by the Trianon Press, 1958. I am grateful to Mr. Arnold Fawcus for his kind cooperation.

Acknowledgment is due the following publishers for permission to quote from their publications: Doubleday & Company, Inc., for *Blake's Apocalypse*, copyright 1963 by Harold Bloom, and *Psyche and Symbol*, copyright 1958 by Violet S. de Laszlo; Columbia University Press, for Robert McQueen Grant's *Gnosticism, a Source Book of Heretical Writings from the Early Christian Period;* Barrie and Rockliff, for Stephen Hobhouse's *Sacred and Mystical Writings of William Law;* Harper and Row, for Aldous Huxley's *The Perennial Philosophy* and John Joseph Stoudt's translation of Jacob Boehme's *The Way to Christ;* Basic Books, Inc., for Lancelot Law Whyte's *The Unconscious Before Freud;* Beacon Press, for *The Gnostic Religion,* copyright 1963 by Hans Jonas; The Nonesuch Press, for Geoffrey Keynes' edition of William Blake's *Poetry and Prose;* George Allen & Unwin, Ltd., for William Kingsland's *The Gnosis or Ancient Wisdom in the Christian Scriptures;* The *London Times Literary Supplement* for "Two Faces of Jung"; W. J. Sloane Associates, William Morrow and Company, copyright 1954, for Edwin Muir's *An Autobiography;* and the Bodley Head, Ltd., for W. P. Witcutt's *Blake: A Psychological Study*.

I wish to thank David V. Erdman and Mrs. Jane Novak for advice and assistance.

# The Book of Urizen

## The Background

William Blake has been said to be, and not to be, a mystic, a pantheist, an occultist, a Neoplatonist, a Swedenborgian, an Arian, and a Christian. Speaking for himself, Blake said that he believed the Bible and professed himself a Christian. But the most superficial reading of Blake's prose and poetry shows him not to have been an institutional Christian nor a fundamentalist reader of the Bible. He thought that it would be a lasting witness against both Jews and Christians that they assumed an exclusive right to the benefits of God; he believed that the word of God was universal and that every man might "converse with God & be a King & Priest in his own house." Blake was catholic but not Catholic; protestant but not Protestant; and not a proponent of Christianity, an organized religion associated with the state, but a believer in what might be called Jesus-sanity, a faith arrived at by the individual conscience.

Perhaps there is no name for his faith. Perhaps he defined himself when, after classifying all men as being either Strong, Beautiful, or Ugly, he described the Strong Man as "a receptacle of Wisdom, a sublime energizer" who "acts from conscious superiority, and marches on in fearless dependance on the divine decrees, raging with the inspirations of a prophetic mind." (See the *Descriptive Catalogue*.)

Such a definition, of course, is so broad as to permit consideration of Blake as either Christian or heretic. But in Blake's opinion, to be a Christian in God's sight entails being a heretic in the Church's. Convinced that this was so, Blake disavowed the Church and affiliated himself with that unorganized "heterodoxical" faith which, despite the Church's constant opposition, has so well maintained its tradition that it deserves recognition as the Other Orthodoxy.

In its comprehensive, faction-encompassing scope, this faith has no name. It cannot be called Protestantism because it protests as much against the respectable Protestant churches as against the Catholic. It cannot be thought of as heresy except in the way that treason is

1

thought treason when it fails to prosper. Yeats referred to it as "heterodox mysticism," but this is a clumsy term and, in its emphasis upon the single element of mysticism, too narrow. Huxley's phrase, The Perennial Philosophy, is as broad as Yeats's is narrow, and equally clumsy.

Perhaps no term will suffice. But among the various alternatives that present themselves, the word *gnosticism* seems to possess the greatest descriptive force. As a religious movement in the early days of the Christian era, Gnosticism enjoyed a moment of influence, but, unable to organize its forces, soon faded out of contention. The movement was aberrational. But the gnostic point of view was not. In his *Great Heresies and Church Councils,* Jean Guitton finds it a way of thinking that has always existed and always will exist, stemming "from a fundamental attitude of the human mind," and notes evidence of its influence upon Philo, Plotinus, Spinoza, and Hegel, among others, upon religions other than the Christian, and, in the twentieth century, upon existentialists, Jungian psychoanalysts, theosophists, and surrealists. [1] Taking the word in this broad sense, gnosticism is not necessarily a philosophical system like Neoplatonism, and a man may be a gnostic without knowing that at one time Gnostics did devise systems. The twentieth-century Gnostic, William Kingsland, says of Boehme that ". . . although uninstructed and uninitiated in any of the Mystery schools—[he] *saw,* by his own natural faculty, those same deep truths which are taught in those Schools." [2]

Blake may or may not have known more of Gnosticism than Boehme did. There is the evidence of Henry Crabb Robinson's comment:

> On my obtaining from him the declaration that the Bible was the Word of God, I referred to the commencement of Genesis—In the Beginning God created the Heavens and the Earth. But I gained nothing by this, for I was triumphantly told [by Blake] that this God was not Jehovah but the Elohim; and the doctrine of the Gnostics repeated with sufficient consistency to silence one so unlearned as myself. [3]

---

1—Pp. 51-79.
2—*The Gnosis or Ancient Wisdom in the Christian Scriptures,* p. 31.
3—Quoted from Arthur Symons, *William Blake,* London, 1907.

2

But Kathleen Raine lightly dismisses Robinson's testimony: "Blake he calls a Gnostic; and it is quite possible that Blake did know something of the Gnostics from the writings of Joseph Priestley and elswhere." [4]

Sloss and Wallis are less cavalier; of *The Book of Urizen* they observe: "What we have here is only a fragment, but it is enough to show that Blake was influenced by a knowledge, not perhaps very accurate or detailed, of Gnostic thought...." (I, 82.) And Damon agrees: "Blake seems to have rediscovered, or perhaps adapted for himself, the Gnostic heresy." (P. 116.) In *William Blake's Circle of Destiny*, M. O. Percival cites many parallels with Gnostic thought.

But a later group of scholars has been engaged in dissociating Blake from esoteric influences. Both Raine and George Mills Harper have been criticized for exaggerating the degree of Blake's debt to Plotinus. Mark Schorer has suggested against earlier assumptions that Blake was "not so much a disciple of Jacob Böhmen and Swedenborg as a fellow visionary." [5] And Harold Bloom is vehement in denying Blake's association with suspect groups of thinkers. In a reference to Section 91 of *Jerusalem*, he says:

> Blake is rejecting all Hermeticism here even as he rejected Swedenborg, Böhmen, and Paracelsus in *The Marriage of Heaven and Hell*. No amount of insistence on this point is likely to stop the continuous flow of writings on Blake's relation to arcane traditions, yet it is hard to see how Blake himself could have been clearer, more emphatic, or more scornful on this subject. A lunatic fringe of enthusiastic occult Blakeans is likely to abide as the left wing of Blake studies until the veritable apocalypse, and all one can do is to counsel students and readers to ignore them. [6]

One can visualize Professor Bloom looming like a senator before his students and brandishing a list of 205 Blake scholars who are card-carrying occultists. It can be argued that, like a senator, he has

---

4—"Blake's Debt to Antiquity," *Sewanee Review*, 71, 429.

5—*William Blake: The Politics of Vision*, p. 122.

6—Harold Bloom, *Blake's Apocalypse*, p. 429.

somewhat overstated his case. Perhaps this can be demonstrated by showing that Blake, denying basic doctrines of Catholicism and Calvinism, could find alternative doctrines, or at least support for such as he himself forged, among adherents to the arcane tradition, feeling free, of course, to reject or modify whatever he disliked or outgrew.

A quick history of Europe from the gnostic point of view takes the following course. When the Christians triumphed in the competition for the soul of man, the successful priestly hierarchy—"crude realists, literalizers, and historicizers . . . quite incapable of understanding the dynamic and flexible teachings of the Gnosis" [7] — subjugated the "civilized" world to a dogmatic theology and a rigid ethic. They burned the Gnostic books and expelled the Knowers as heretics, thus plunging Europe into the ignorance, superstition, and bigotry of the pre-Renaissance centuries.

Realizing that this was merely Karma and had to run its course, the Gnostic Resistance went underground, where, as an organization possessing a body of thought, an art, a literature, it ceased to exist. But the spirit remained, manifesting itself here in a Meister Eckhart, elsewhere in Kabbalists, Neoplatonists, orientalists, theosophists, and alchemists. And eventually the patient fortitude of the faithful had its reward, for the humanists of the Platonic Academy, "messing up Christian and Pagan mysticism, allegory, occultism, demonology, Trismegistus, Psellus, Porphyry, into a most eloquent and exciting and exhilarating botch-patch — 'did for' the mediaeval fear of the *dies irae* and for human abasement generally." [8]

The Renaissance humanists did not identify themselves as Gnostics. No Gnostic Church existed for them to join. Yet it might with some justification be said that, because they were vouchsafed a revelation of the Knowledge and were in good faith and in the state of gnostic grace, they belonged "invisibly to the Church." Their anti-

---

7—Kingsland, p. 48.

8—Ezra Pound, *The New Age, a weekly Review of Politics, Literature and Art,* (11 Feb. 1915), p. 409.

scholasticism, anti-clericalism, anti-nomianism, neo-paganism, Faustian aspiration, [9] and belief in salvation through knowledge instead of faith made them unwitting members.

Theirs was a famous victory; but only a battle, not the war, was won. Protestantism not only wrote Presbyter larger than Priest but Pentateuch larger than Penates; nationalism made kings divine; commercialism and capitalism imposed the more subtle but more powerful and durable tyranny of conformity to the code of Respectability, enjoining the will to produce and the desire to possess material things; science and technology forced philosophy's shrinkage to her second cause. (Not the composition of *Paradise Lost* but the organization of the Royal Society and the founding of the Bank of England epitomize the late seventeenth century's legacy to the modern world.) [10]

Prophets were needed as before. And they were available. In Germany, Jacob Boehme (1575-1624) successfully rose above the hysterical condemnations of the orthodox to exert an influence beyond his place and time; in England, the Cambridge Platonists, the Quakers, such individuals as Robert Fludd chipped away at Catholic, Anglican, and Calvinist dogmas. In eighteenth-century England when (despite them) Anglicanism had been established as the State Church, and when Locke and Newton had given Deism its "scientific" support, William Law (an Anglican, but with a difference) reacted by translating Boehme; other dissidents brought Swedenborg's works to bear. The philosophy was, as Huxley says, perennial.

---

9—"It is of interest, though in a context far removed from ours, that in Latin surroundings Simon used the cognomen *Faustus* ("the favored one"): this in connection with his permanent cognomen "the Magician" and the fact that he was accompanied by a Helen of Troy shows clearly that we have here one of the sources of the Faust legend of the early Renaissance. Surely few admirers of Marlowe's and Goethe's plays have an inkling that their hero is the descendant of a gnostic sectary, and that the beautiful Helen called up by his art was once the fallen Thought of God through whose raising mankind was to be saved." Hans Jonas, *The Gnostic Religion*, p. 111.

10—As for the eighteenth century's contribution, Yeats spoke to the point when he ascribed the loss of the Early Paradise to God's taking a spinning-jenney out of Locke's side.

Since the Ancient Wisdom tends toward Yea-saying—affirming freedom of thought, individualism, and a tolerant morality [11] — it has found significant adherents among the European poets. Denis Saurat lists Spenser, Milton, Blake, Shelley, Emerson, Whitman, Goethe, Heine, Wagner, Nietzsche, Hugo, de Vigny, Lamartine, and Leconte de Lisle among them. [12] In our time, Yeats, Pound, Lawrence, Gide, Huxley, and others might be added to the list.

Of all these perhaps none was to such a degree dedicated to the tradition of heterodoxy as Blake. [13] His sensualism, his visionary experience, his despisal of authority, his energetic, questioning intellect, his esemplastic imagination turned him against "orthodoxy" in any form. He joined the Liberty Boys in supporting political revolution, was vehement against academicism in the world of art, removed himself further from "neoclassicism" in poetry than any other contemporary poet, opposed those intellectual movements (*e.g.*, science and Deism) which de-personalized and Nature-alized God or (*e.g.*, Catholicism, Anglicanism, and Calvinism) dogmatized and monopolized the Christian faith.

All this found expression in his early poems, and most excitingly in *The Marriage of Heaven and Hell*, a kind of manifesto unimpeded by the exigencies of narrative structure and uncluttered by the inventions of his myth-making faculty. But having made his declaration of rights and wrongs, Blake turned his mind to the First and Last Things, seeking answers to the eternal questions of Whence, Why, Whither. His answers, or, rather, his explorations toward answers, were embodied in a series of epic poems. *The Book of Urizen* is the first of his attempts at cosmogonic myth.

Cosmogony is concerned with the questions of how and why the universe came to be as it is; how and why man—and woman—came

---

11—This last was not altogether the case with the original Gnostics. One branch did indeed advocate libertinism, but another preached contempt of the world.

12—Denis Saurat, *Literature and Occult Tradition*, p. 6. Saurat's position has been challenged but not by any means disposed of.

13—It must be understood that this is really a way of saying that Blake was (as Kathleen Raine puts it) "a traditionalist in a society that had as a whole lapsed from tradition."

to be as they are; how and why "evil" came to be; how and when man may escape that evil.

The Old and New Testaments, of course, have provided answers, and, for some millions of Europeans, the only answers, since the Jewish writings (and only they) were thought to contain the revealed Word of God. The early Gnostics, however, though they recognized that the Scriptures conveyed significant truths, denied them both a monopoly on Truth and the glory of being a revelation. The Wisdom, they argued, was discovered by man, not revealed to him, and had been known to men long before a word of the Bible had been written. The Jewish account of the Creation was, to their way of thinking, a borrowing from less primitive peoples and a retelling in forms suited to the limited intelligence of the Jews. Read literally, the Jewish account is scientifically untrue; read allegorically, it is philosophically unsophisticated; read apologetically, it has been used (by Jews and Christians) to foster the evil concept of a "chosen people" knowing the one God, entrusted with the one Law.

Centuries later, the Renaissance trinity of Humanism, Scientism, and Reformationism supplied both the motives and the means of returning to this early Gnostic position. But many, and these among the best, did not welcome the opportunity. Milton, for example, saw through the optic glass, but only darkly, and lacking the exalted clarity of vision which results when Love and Wisdom cooperate, to see as one, he misdoubted what he saw. His wavering between the new and the old astronomy was only symptomatic of the deeper self-dividedness, shown so clearly in his major works. A Blakean description of Milton might run as follows: by nature a sensualist, he glorified chastity in *Comus;* fierce individualist, he made strict obedience the cardinal virtue in *Paradise Lost;* cosmopolitan humanist, he approved murderous intolerance in his tracts; freeborn English rebel against alien authority, he chose the strict Aristotelian tragic structure instead of the free and native Shakespearean in *Samson Agonistes,* and in his works in general tortured English on a Latin rack. In view of this never-ending battle within himself between Satan and Jehovah, it is no wonder that all his major works are stories of temptations. Or that the character most like himself fell farthest. Or

7

that, though Jehovah regularly wins, Satan has the best lines. Milton was (as Blake saw) of the gnostic party, but his mind denied what his heart affirmed. Never in his life did he bring together *L'Allegro* and *Il Penseroso* as Blake did Innocence and Experience.

Seen from a gnostic point of view, Milton had, in his sevententh-century incarnation, achieved a higher level of knowledge than most, but he had failed to arrive at the total Wisdom. It was left for Blake, in *Milton,* to show him in another incarnation achieving that consummation. It was also left for Blake to revise the false cosmogony which Milton had so powerfully delineated in *Paradise Lost.*

In line with the taste of our present anti-mythological age, twentieth-century Gnostics sometimes express their cosmogonical theories in plain prose. William Kingsland, for example, orders things thus:

> The cosmic aspect of religion is this — Humanity as a whole is a Unitary Cosmic Entity associated with the cosmic function of this particular globe as a unit in the Solar System: that System being a still larger cosmic unit whose life-history is represented by the Sun; or, spiritually, by the Solar Logos.

> The great cycle of Man's evolution on this globe is a "fall" and a recovery; an *outgoing* from Spirit into Matter, and a *return* to Spirit.

> Humanity reaches forward to a spiritual consummation when the whole Earth will be peopled with a Race of men fully conscious of their god-like nature and powers; and, sin, sickness, and death will have been banished for the remaining period of the Earth's cosmic cycle.

> The Cosmic Process is an *outgoing* from the ONE, and a *return* thereto; and Man—like everything else in the Cosmos —must return to his Source. It is the great Cosmic systole and diastole, called in the East the Days and Nights of Brahma.

> If, then, Religion is for us as individuals the finding of the real spiritual Self—that transcendental Self which is the

root and source of all these temporary *appearances* which are our little temporary personal selves—so also is it with Humanity as a whole; for it is our attainment as individuals which gradually accomplishes the attainment of Humanity in its *cosmic* aspect. [14]

Huxley, not, like Kingsland, a paid-up member but a fringe-dweller, expresses it in more general philosophical terms:

*Philosophia Perennis* — the phrase was coined by Leibniz: but the thing — the metaphysic that recognizes a divine Reality substantial to the world of things and lives and minds; the psychology that finds in the soul something similar to, or even identical with, divine Reality; the ethic that places man's final end in the knowledge of the imma-nent and transcendent Ground of all being — the thing is immemorial and universal. [15]

But the early Gnostics relied on a combination of myth and allegory. Irenaeus's account of the Barbelo-Gnostic doctrine shows a characteristic Gnostic Genesis:

There is a never-ageing Aeon in a Virginal Spirit which is called Barbelo; the unnameable Father is also there. He wished to reveal himself to Barbelo. This Thought came forth and stood in his sight and asked for Foreknowledge. When Foreknowledge had also come forth, then they both requested Imperishability, and she came forth; then Eternal Life. Barbelo rejoiced in them and, looking towards the Greatness and delighting in the Conception, she bore a Light like it. This was the beginning of the illumination and gene-ration of all things.

When the Father saw this Light he anointed it with his own goodness so that it would be perfect. This is Christ ["anointed"]. He then asked that a helper, Mind, be given him, and Mind came forth. Then the Father emitted Logos. Next there were unions of Thought and Logos, Imperish-

14—*Op. cit.*, pp. 71-72.

15—Aldous Huxley, *The Perennial Philosophy,* p. vii.

ability and Christ; Eternal Life was joined with Will and Mind with Foreknowledge. These emanations magnified the great Light and Barbelo. Afterwards, from Thought and Logos was emitted Self-Born as a representation of the great Light; it was greatly honoured and all things were subjected to it. With it was emitted Truth, and thus there was another pair; Self-Born and Truth. From the light which is Christ and from Imperishability four luminaries were emitted to stand about Self-Born; again from Will and Eternal Life four emissions took place to serve the four luminaries which are called Grace, Willing, Intelligence, and Thinking. Grace was united with the great first Light, which is Saviour and is called Armogen; Willing with the second, called Raguel; Intelligence, with the third, called David; Thinking with the fourth, called Eleleth. When all of these had been established, Self-Born also emitted the Perfect and True Man, who is also called Adamas because he is adamant, as his sources are, though he was separated from the first Light by Armogen. Perfect Knowledge was emitted by Self-Born along with the Man, and was joined to him; from her he knows the one who is above all. Unconquered Power was given him by the Virginal Spirit in which all things rest to praise the great Aeon.

Thus were revealed the Mother, the Father, and the Son; from the Man and Knowledge was born the Tree, which is also called Knowledge [gnosis].

Then from the first angel which is with Monogenes [Self-Born] was emitted Holy Spirit, which is also called Sophia and Prunicos. When this spirit saw that all the rest had partners but she did not, she sought someone with whom to be united. When she found none, she was extended and looked down to the lower regions in the belief that she would find one there. When she found none, she leaped back, wearied because she had made this effort without the good will of the Father. Afterwards, driven by simplicity and kindness, she generated a work in which were Ignorance and Presumption. This work is called Proarchon, the fashioner of this universe. He stole a great power from his mother and departed from her to the lower regions and made the firmament of heaven, in which he dwells. And since he is Ignorance, he made the powers beneath him: angels, firmaments, and everything earthly. Then he was united with Presumption and generated Wickedness, Jealousy, Envy, Strife, and Desire. When they were generated, the Mother Sophia fled in grief and withdrew above; she became the Eight for those who count from below. When she withdrew, he thought he was alone, and therefore he said, "I am a jealous God, and there is none but me." [16]

Readers of such a passage will immediately divide into two groups. There will be those who agree to the *Britannica's* declaration that here is a religion in which "the determining forces were a fantastic oriental imagination and a sacramentalism which degenerated into the wildest superstitions" and will with no small relief return from its rain-forest myth to the sublime simplicity of *Genesis* and the humanness of *Paradise Lost*. But there will also be those who will regret the loss at least of the myth if not of the religion as well. Hans Jonas is so eloquent in *his* sense of loss that he deserves extended quotation:

Out of the mist of the beginning of our era there looms a pageant of mythical figures whose vast, superhuman contours might people the walls and ceiling of another Sistine Chapel. Their countenances and gestures, the roles in which they are cast, the drama which they enact, would yield images different from the biblical ones on which the imagination of the beholder was reared, yet strangely familiar to him and disturbingly moving. The stage would be the same, the theme as transcending; the creation of the world, the destiny of man, fall and redemption, the first and last things. But how much more numerous would be the cast, how much more bizarre the symbolism, how much more extravagant the emotions! Almost all the action would be in the heights, in the divine or angelic or daimonic realm, a drama of pre-cosmic persons in the supranatural world, of which the drama of man in the natural world is but a distant echo. And yet that transcendental drama before all time, depicted in the actions and passions of manlike figures,

16—Robert McQueen Grant, *Gnosticism, a Source Book of Heretical Writings from the Early Christian Period*, pp. 49-51.

would be of intense human appeal: divinity tempted, unrest stirring among the blessed Aeons, God's erring Wisdom, the Sophia, falling prey to her folly, wandering in the void and darkness of her own making, endlessly searching, lamenting, suffering, repenting, laboring her passion into matter, her yearning into soul; a blind and arrogant Creator, believing himself the Most High and lording it over the creation, the product, like himself, of fault and ignorance; the Soul, trapped and lost in the labyrinth of the world, seeking to escape and frightened back by the gatekeepers of the cosmic prison, the terrible archons; a Savior from the Light beyond venturing into the nether world, illumining the darkness, opening a path, healing the divine breach: a tale of light and darkness, of knowledge and ignorance, of serenity and passion, of conceit and pity, on the scale not of man but of eternal beings that are not exempt from suffering and error. [17]

It seems to me beyond question that Blake would have agreed with Jonas rather than with the *Britannica*.

First, if anything is clear about Blake it is that he was not satisfied with the sublime simplicity of the *Genesis* story. His prophetic poems are as fantastically imaginative as anything the Sethian-Ophites or Barbelo-Gnostics conceived. And they are so because he did not find the simple Biblical myth adequate to his experience. For one thing, the Bible's failure to give a motive for the creation did not satisfy his questioning mind; for another, the concept of a creation which *precedes* a Fall seemed to him neither as philosophically profound nor as psychologically probable as a creation which is itself the Fall, nor did it satisfactorily explain the suffering in the animal world. His rejection of a creation by a transcendent deity's fiat in favor of a creation occurring through the manifestation in cosmic plurality of a previously unmanifested Unity forced him into the most intricate complications of cause and effect.

Second, however he esteemed Milton and however much he steeped himself in Milton's poetry, he did not accept his concept of God, his explanation of the creation, nor his account of the subse-

---

17—Hans Jonas, *op. cit.*, p. xiii.

quent Fall. Nor are his versions of paradise lost and regained humanized in the way that Milton's are. In *Paradise Lost,* how all-too-manlike are the ostensibly superhuman characters in appearance, motivation, speech, and act, how down-to-earth God's kingly court and the battle between the angels. Even Hell is visualizable in human terms. Only Satan's meeting with Sin and Death has an element of strangeness. We can find a local habitation in almost any part of Milton's poem. And in *Paradise Regained,* how wistfully human is the Jesus who, thinking of Quintius, Fabricius, Curius, and Regulus, aspires to "Accomplish what they did, perhaps, and more." In Blake's epics, we are in another world, meeting characters whose conduct is exotically supra-human. Blake could have felt a sense of familiarity with the early Gnostic writings as Milton could never have done. He had their kind of myth-making faculty.

Blake, then, has both the intellectual individualism and the fertile mythological imagination which characterized the Gnostics. But does he, beyond this, echo (whether wittingly or no is beside the point) any of their fundamental doctrines?

The answer is affirmative. The Gnostics, though they varied in specific points, tended to agree in the following general beliefs:

1. They posited an original spiritual unity which came to be split into a plurality.

2. As a result of this pre-cosmic division the universe was created. It was created by a leader possessing inferior spiritual powers, a leader often having the appearance of the Old Testament Jehovah.

3. A female emanation from God was involved in the cosmic creation.

4. In the cosmos, space and time have a malevolently spiritual character and may be personified as demonic beings separating man from God.

5. For man, the universe is a vast prison. He is enslaved both by the physical laws of nature and by such psychic laws as the Mosaic Code.

6. Mankind may be personified as Adam, who lies in the deep sleep of ignorance, his powers of spiritual self-awareness stupefied by materiality.

7. However, within each natural man is an "inner man." This is a fallen spark of the divine substance. Since within each man this spark of holiness exists, the possibility of an awakening from the present stupefaction exists.

8. What effects the awakening is not obedience, not faith, not good works, but knowledge.

9. Before the awakening, men undergo troubled dreams.

10. The knowledge that awakens man from these dreams is not arrived at by cognition but through revelationary experience, and it is not an accession of information but a modification of the sensate being.

11. The awakening (that is, the salvation) of any individual is a cosmic event.

12. Since the whole universal effort is to restore the wholeness and unity of the godhead, active rebellion against the moral law of the Old Testament is enjoined upon every man.

How does the Blakean teaching accord with these points of doctrine? There are remarkable resemblances. In Blake, an original spiritual unity is split; the universe is created and ruled by a figure resembling Jehovah; a female emanation is involved; space and time are personified; man is enslaved by natural law and Mosaic law; humanity is personified by an Adam-like figure who lies asleep; within the natural man is the spiritual man who can be awakened to salvation; the awakening occurs when four-fold vision (spiritual

14

knowledge) is achieved; dreams trouble sleepers; the four-fold vision is not scientific knowledge but spiritual understanding; when a given man awakens, he undergoes a Last Judgment; the fulfillment of desire, action against Thou Shalt Nots, is enjoined upon every man.

Suppose that Blake had never heard of Gnosticism; where could he have found support for his heterodox concepts? From the Neoplatonists, as Raine and Harper have pointed out. From Jacob Boehme, who declared that

> The whole Christian religion consists in this: that we learn to know ourselves, what we are, whence we have come, how we have departed *from the unity and entered into the multiplicity* . . .; [18]

who believed that the Christian needs no church ("the saint has his church with him and within him at all places"), no priest or preacher, no sacraments; who professed the Christian to be non-sectarian ("He can live among the sects . . . and will not be attached to any. He has only one doctrine and that is, Christ within him") [19]; and who found heaven and hell married within the individual:

> If our conversation is in heaven, then heaven must be within us. Christ lives in heaven and if we are His Temple, then that same heaven must be within us.

> But since sin nevertheless attacks us in our being, by which the Devil in us has access to us, then hell also must be within us, because the Devil lives in hell. [20]

Originally, Boehme says, man had a trichotomous soul. When the properties of all three "stood in equal concordance," man enjoyed a paradisal state, standing in heaven as well as in the external world. [21] But in due course this "coincidence of contraries" was disrupted so that one dominated over the others, and Adam fell into a deep sleep — that is, fell from divine Harmony "into the aroused

18—*The Way to Christ*, trans. John Joseph Stoudt, p. 108. Italics mine.
19—*Ibid.*, p. 105.
20—*Ibid.*, p. 79.
21—*Ibid.*, pp. 84-85.

properties of evil and good."[22] In this condition, Adam no longer had the magical power of bearing his kind "out of himself without tearing and opening his body and spirit." Nor was he any longer androgynous. God took Adam's egocentric love and fashioned it into Eve. Henceforth both Adam and Eve had "members for animal reproduction" and earthly guts. They came to know shame and vanity and so "died to the Kingdom of Heaven and woke up in the external world; then the fair seal of holy Vitality and Character died to God's Love and awoke instead in the grim wrath, *i.e.,* in the dark fire-world." [23]

The "grim wrath of God." The doctrine of God's wrath is fundamental to Boehme and finds various expression in his writings. He can, as Hobhouse says, *"seem* to support the evil theory that Jesus dies on the cross to appease the wrath of an angry Father, and *seem* to suggest that God is essentially a wrathful God: 'The wrath and the anger, together with the abyss of hell, stand in the center of the Father.' " [24] But elsewhere Boehme will exclaim: "In God there is no anger, there is pure love." It is the unmanifested God who is pure love. But manifestation cannot occur without the interaction of opposites. Therefore:

Unless there be a *contrarium* in God, there would be no form or distinction . . . . For every divine, good power has in the foundation of hell, that is, in the *No,* a contrarium or opposite . . . . in order that the Yes or truth may be known. And here the two strong kingdoms of the eternity are to be seen, which have been in strife with one another and are always so; and *the strife continueth to eternity for it is also from eternity,* between the fierceness and the meekness. If the fierceness were not, there could be no mobility. . . . The fierceness or wrath is the root of all things . . . without it there could be no enmity, but all would be a nothing . . .

---

22—*Ibid.,* p. 87.

23—*Ibid.,* p. 89.

24—Stephen Hobhouse, ed. *Sacred and Mystical Writings of William Law,* p. 369; *cf.* Blake: "First God Almighty comes with a Thump on the Head. Then Jesus Christ comes with a balm to heal it." ("Vision of the Last Judgement.")

all things would be one thing, and all merely God . . . in a sweet meekness. But where would be the mobility, the Kingdom, the power and the glory? Therefore we have often said, 'The anger is the root of life, and if it be without the light, then it is not God, but hell fire; but if the light shines therein, it becomes paradise and fulness of joy.' [25]

William Law, the eighteenth-century English mystic who popularized Boehme's doctrines in England and through whom Blake apparently learned of the German's thought, de-emphasized the element of wrath in the God-head. According to Law, there is, first, "an abyssal, unsearchable, triune God"; second, there is his manifestation of "beatific visibility and outward glory"—Eternal Nature, or "the heavenly Jerusalem"; and, third, there is the temporary nature in which man lives and which is "nothing else but eternal nature separated, divided, compacted, made visible and changeable for a time . . . ."[26]

The Eternal Nature was brought to being "in and by and through the glorious union of eternal fire, and light, and spirit"— that is, the Father, Son, and Holy Spirit. It was "the goodness of God breaking forth into a desire to communicate good" which was the "cause and the beginning of the creation." [27]

God created angels out of that eternal nature so that they had "fire, and light, and spirit, as the triune glory of their created being." Those could have become fixed in this glory, and some did. But not Lucifer. Since light is born of fire, and spirit is born of fire and light, and since will must precede and cause birth, Lucifer and his cohorts of angels were enabled to will a separation from God, producing a ruined section within the Eternal Nature.

Out of these ruins God made a second creation—that of a temporary nature which "stands in its state of war, a war betwixt the fire and pride of fallen angels and the meekness and humility of the

25—*Ibid.*, p. 370.
26—*Ibid.*, p. 45.
27—*Ibid.*, p. 71.

Lamb of God." [28] And Adam, who, like Lucifer, could have remained fixed in his glory, did not but willed the knowledge of temporal nature and so lost the "light and spirit of Heaven for the light and spirit of this world." [29]

The keyword in all this is *separation*. Law states it very plainly:

> . . . there is no evil, no guilt, no deformity in any creature, but in its dividing and separating itself from something which God had given to be in union with it. This, and this alone, is the whole nature of all good and evil in the creature, both in the moral and spiritual world, in spiritual and material things. [30]

Thus it may be said that "as the devil is nothing but a fire-spirit broken off from its angelical light and glory, so hell is nothing but the fire of heaven separated from its first light and majesty." [31]

It is equally a division of powers in man that leads him astray. He, like all that exists, has spiritual properties which can be eternal and infinitely perfect. They are so in God and should be so in man, but "in the creature, being limited and finite, they may be divided and separated from one another by the creature itself." [32] These heavenly properties are filled with a desire to return to their heavenly state. Thus Law can say enthusiastically that "our desire is all, it does all, and governs all, and all that we have and are must arise from it. . . ." [33]

In addition to desire, man's power derives from imagination and will. It is these which "communicate with eternity. . . ." [34] Hobhouse comments on Law's triumvirate:

---

28—*Ibid.*, p. 107.

29—*Ibid.*, p. 47.

30—*Ibid.*, p. 39.

31—*Ibid.*, p. 50.

32—*Ibid.*, p. 39.

33—*Ibid.*, p. 53.

34—*Ibid.*

This trinity of faculties unlike the traditional "understanding, will, and memory" is directly derived from Boehme and forms the basis of his psychology. To him desire represents the untrammelled, impersonal, blind, and aimless forces that lie at the bottom of all that is. These forces produce nevertheless their contrary in the form of an image-shaping energy, and positive and negative together become embodied in a personal will, which is the centre and germ and driving force of all life. [35]

Law more than any other English writer of importance was infused with Boehme's ideas. But his thought did not coincide with Boehme's. There is no way of knowing how much of Blake's thought was directed or colored by Boehme, or by Boehme as modified by Law. Certainly his thought did not coincide with that of either —just as Yeats's thought is at a far remove from Blake's, though he assisted in the editing of Blake's work and was admittedly as open to his influence as, say, Leda to the swan's. (The four conflicting powers that Yeats finds influencing each man resemble yet significantly differ from Blake's. Yeats's idea that the human soul "would not be conscious were it not suspended between contraries" is Blakean, but Yeats's historical extrapolation of the idea is his own.)

Such considerations are of no particular account. Blake, individualist, libertarian, sensualist, and visionary, naturally read authors whose interests and attitudes were similar to his own, thinkers who were members of the Other Orthodoxy. Those he read had no monopoly on the ideas they expressed. They were, as Blake came to be, merely significant (and idiosyncratic) utterers of a body of thought which had existed for centuries and would continue to exist into the twentieth century.

Generally speaking, all that he needed to arrive at his religious position (and to find the symbols to express it) was the Bible and a sufficient knowledge of the Christian tradition. But in Blake's case a sufficient knowledge of the tradition included knowledge both of the dogmas and of the heresies that they generated. And Blake being

---

35—*Ibid.*, p. 253.

what he was, his sympathies extended rather more to the heretics than to the authoritarians. His reading in the earlier rebels expedited and colored but did not necessarily initiate or control his thought. However, even cursory examination of the preceding quotations discovers words and ideas that became prominent in Blake's poems: for example, the location of Christ and heaven and hell in man; the interrelation of fire and light or wrath and joy; the opposition of contraries; the egocentric separation, and the destruction of a concordance of powers; the loss of the androgynous state; the naming of eternal nature as "Jerusalem"; the idea of humanity as the One Man; the emphasis upon desire and imagination; the requirement that Jesus die to appease an angry Jehovah's wrath.

There are, on the other hand, two specific things that he would not have done had he not read his predecessors: had he not read *Paradise Lost,* he would not have written *Milton;* had he not read Swedenborg, he would not have written *The Marriage of Heaven and Hell.* Each of these works was written in specific reaction against a man some of whose teaching he admired, some of which he rejected. In *Milton* he shows the earlier poet in the process of correcting his influential errors. No such second chance is given Swedenborg. Yet it would be an error to argue that such of the Swedish mystic's ideas as Blake found congenial were incontinently expunged from the latter's mind when he wrote *The Marriage.* He rejected what he believed to be false, modified what he thought to be imprecise, assimilated what he felt to be true.

This was his course when he came to write *The Book of Urizen.* It is not a Christian poem, but it contains elements of Biblical lore; it revises Milton's creation story but borrows (sometimes for satirical purposes) from *Paradise Lost;* it indicates Blake's knowledge both of Neoplatonic and of Gnostic myth but projects Blake's own; its underlying philosophy has affinities with that of Boehme and that of Swedenborg, but only affinities. It is, in short, Blake's original contribution to the literature of the Other Orthodoxy.

20

# The Poem

In 1794, Blake, having written his tracts against orthodox Christianity, Deism, puritanism, rationalism, political conservatism, moral hyprocisy, and the like, set about writing his books of revelations. The first of these is *The Book of Urizen,* a narrative poem, perhaps intended to be of epic proportions but left both fragmentary and unrevised, ostensibly portraying by means of symbolic characters the creation of the cosmos.

E. D. Hirsch has recently argued that Blake is *not* concerned with the creation of the cosmos but with the spiritual failure of man, a failure which Blake externalizes and dramatizes by writing a parody of cosmological works. Hirsch believes that Blake did not write a genuine cosmological work until he embarked upon *Jerusalem.* Harold Bloom thinks the poem primarily a satire of earlier creation accounts and only secondarily a serious cosmogonical effort of his own. Much earlier, S. Foster Damon had read it both as a cosmic drama dealing with a creation which, being a Fall, initiates the problem of evil in the universe, and as a psychic drama, a study of the fall from innocence which each man experiences.

As I see it, the poem is an account of Blake's own fall from innocence, an account which, since each man creates hell and heaven within himself, can be used as a workable hypothesis to explain the cosmic creation. It is therefore primarily a psychological study and secondarily a serious cosmogonical effort. Since it is also a narrative working within a tradition, it employs characters who must perforce resemble in attributes and actions the characters of earlier similar narratives, particularly Genesis and *Paradise Lost.* But since Blake's myth runs counter to that of these antecedents (the assumed God being a destroyer rather than a creator), every borrowed attribute and action contains an implicit irony. The poem is therefore, thirdly, a satire.

That Blake is challenging traditional concepts is at once made evident by the metre he has chosen to employ. His basic line, the trimeter, and his basic rhythm, anapestic, are as far as anything can

far from Milton's blank verse

be from Milton's blank verse. Every eighteenth-century blank-verse writer lay under Milton's shadow; it would have been impossible for Blake, treating, as he was, a similar theme, to have been his own man in that verse form. To choose so short a line and so lilting a rhythm for so great an argument also constituted a challenge to himself. Could he rework the pretty measure of

> A flower was offered to me
> Such a flower as May never bore . . .

to make it a suitable vehicle for the titanic labors he was engaged in describing? He did, to such a degree that one is rarely aware of the basic rhythm. To begin with, the poem demands to be read first for its meaning and only second for its rhythm, so that the rhythm is transmuted into cadence. Focus upon image and idea must be so concentrated that one forgets the metrical arrangement of the words. Compare the couplet above with

> And a roof, vast petrific around,
> On all sides He fram'd: like a womb.

(The first of these lines is, in addition, made to seem twice its length by the expanding vowels and by the felt need to pause three times— the pause after *vast* in particular muting the rhythm.)

Blake's variations throughout the poem are emphatic: trochees ("Groaning! gnashing! groaning!"), dactyls ("Ages on ages roll'd over him!"), iambs ("He watch'd in shuddring fear"), spondees ("Of beast, bird, fish, serpent & element") work havoc with any sense of expectancy that has been built up. Run-ons are sometimes violent, as in

> First I fought with the fire; consum'd
> Inwards . . . .
>
> — — — —
>
> And self balanc'd stretch'd o'er the void
> I alone, even I! the winds merciless
> Bound . . . .
>
> — — — —
>
> A nerveless silence his prophetic voice
> Siez'd . . . .

And the multiplicity of powerful verbs and participles describing psychic or physical anguish helps to distract attention from prosodic techniques:

> Los smitten with astonishment
> Frightened at the hurtling bones
>
> And at the surging sulphureous
> Perturbed Immortal mad raging.

And yet, underneath it all, is to be sensed that childish lilt— "Then I went to my Pretty Rose-tree"—recalling the divine harmony that has been lost but which, since it exists eternally, can be regained. The poem is nothing if not a prosodic *tour de force*.

The setting for the poem's macrocosmic action is, variously, Eternity, the Void, and Nature.

The characters are (in order of appearance):

1. The Eternals: referred to as *myriads of Eternity, sons of Eternity, the wisdom and joy of life.*

2. Urizen (a deviant member of the Eternals): referred to as *the primeval Priest, Demon, dark power, self-contemplating shadow, the Immortal, that solitary one, the dark Demon, a clod of clay, Perturbed Immortal, the Immortal.*

3. Terrible monsters: referred to as *Sin-bred, seven deadly sins of the soul, living creations, self-begotten armies.*

4. Los (an Eternal chosen to keep watch over the erring Urizen): referred to as *the eternal Prophet.*

5. Enitharmon (an emanation out of Los): referred to as *Pity, female form, first female, divided image.*

6. Orc (Los's likeness begotten on his own divided image): referred to as a *Worm, a serpent, an Infant form, a man child, the Human Shadow, the Child.*

7. The Dead: referred to as *all things.*

8. The Enormous Race (borne by Enitharmon): referred to only in stanza 10 of Chap. VII—unless they equate with the "forms of life" that Urizen meets in the succeeding chapter. (This seems unlikely.)

9. Forms of life (all the dead things—see 7—now awakened to life): referred to (in Chapter I) as *shapes of beast, bird, fish, serpent,* and *element, combustions, blast, vapour,* and *cloud;* generally (in Chapter 8) as *cruel enormities, vast enormities, portions of life, similitudes, mischievous dread terrors, eternal creations, sons and daughters of sorrow, all his race, inhabitants of those cities, reptile forms, remaining sons, brethren;* and specifically (in Chapter 8) as *Thiriel, Utha, Grodna,* and *Fuzon* (the four elements).

10. A female in embryo: referred to as *a cold shadow, a Web, the Net of Religion.*

The story is as follows:

Before the beginning, before Time and Space were, there was a dynamic unity of an unspecified number of eternal energies. It was not an undifferentiated One; nor was it a loose collocation of varied entities. It was what Lavater called Beauty — "the MOST VARIED ONE, THE MOST UNITED VARIETY." [36] It was before the beginning, is now — at least potentially — and ever shall be, world without end, but being inconceivable, it is inexpressible, save by analogy.

One way of visualizing it is as a human body in which all the various parts unselfconsciously work in harmony together. There are brain, heart, loins, and skeletal structure, each quite different from the other, all, however, forming One Man. There are reason, imagination, passion, and instinct, each serving its peculiar spiritual func-

---

36—Geoffrey Keynes' edition of William Blake's *Poetry and Prose,* p. 916.

tion, all united as a Four-in-One, [37] in a state of mutual giving and receiving, a state in which each, moved by the desire to give of his bounty, continually dies deaths of self-sacrifice to be re-vitalized by the others' givings. The One Man does not know himself as merely a Unity nor as merely a Variety. His senses can be either expanded or contracted. When they are expanded, he sees himself as the One who comprises Many; when they are contracted, as the Many comprising the One. That is, he can see himself in his totality; he can also recognize the minute particulars of which the totality is made. [38]

Thus this One Man (who is the "myriads of Eternity") is characterized by infinite comprehension, infinite energy, infinite love, and infinite freedom.

But infinite freedom for every part of the whole means no less than that any part can remove from the whole. Given infinite energy, any one of the major powers might, using the means of contraction, so narrow its infinite comprehension as to lose sight of the totality in its preoccupation with its own particularity. This occurring, infinite love becomes contracted to self-love.

---

37—However, in this poem Blake does not delineate a Four-fold division of Eternity. There are "myriads of Eternity" but only *two* are named—Urizen and Los. In Swedenborg there are also two contraries—Wisdom and Love. Wisdom combines the various ordering powers; Love the desiring, energetic ones. The inference that Blake has not moved far from Swedenborg seems tenable.

38—The theosophist Fabre d'Olivet has an interesting analogue to this theory. Postulating Adam as *man* conceived *abstractly* and Eve as his creative faculty who becomes his material life "making everything within him and without him," he understands Cain and Abel as "the two primordial forces of elementary nature." He describes them thus:

Cain can be conceived as the action of compressive force, and Abel that of expansive force. These two actions, issues of the same source, are hostile from the moment of their birth, according to the manner by which everything exists in nature. They act incessantly the one upon the other, and seek reciprocally to dominate, and to be reduced to their own nature. The compressive action, more energetic than the expansive action, always gains the ascendancy in the beginning; and overwhelming it, so to speak, compacts the universal substance upon which it acts, and gives existence to material forms that were not previously.

Fabre d'Olivet, trans. *Cain* by Lord Byron, pp. 27-8.

That is to say, Eternity is not a stasis but a process. The powers are not alike; they are contraries in constant dialectical opposition producing progressive movement by maintaining a dynamic equilibrium. But if one of the powers endeavors to isolate itself from its contrary, the dialectical process is altered, the dynamic equilibrium destroyed. It is as though one wing of a bird decided not to co-operate with its opposite fellow. Or, more aptly, since Eternity is like a human being, as if the head decided to detach itself from the lower members of the body and go it alone. In either case there would be a Fall.

Wisdom is not *per se* evil; nor is Imagination (or Love) [39] in and of itself good. There is no need to import such moralistic terms at all. The fact is this: when these two (and the other powers with them) collaborate, Eternity *is*, as a variegated but undivided state; when they do not collaborate, Eternity still is—but malfunctioning because divided as well as variegated. It is always there, as an engine is still there, though, because the timer is askew, it operates fitfully. An adjustment will at once produce the Harmony — the radical Innocence — which is Eternity.

Something like this is what Blake is putting into narrative form, using "humanized" figures to represent that Family of Eternal Powers. One member of the Family wearied of the continued activity of desire to give, of constant self-sacrifice, and drew away from his compeers, leaving a void. Altogether self-concerned, he was a new thing, an *unknown* factor (in Chapter I, Blake repeats the word *unknown* five times) in the "annals" of Eternity. Separated from the other Eternals, he sought, so to speak, to save himself by finding his Self. Instead, finding his Self, he lost his reality, becoming a shadow in a vacuum. He was no longer the Ur-Reason, the Our Reason of Eternity, but Your Reason, a thing apart bounded by his self-made Horizon.

---

39—In my view, Los combines the functions of love and imagination in this poem.

Contemplating himself, he changed his function from qualitative synthesis to quantitative analysis, spinning out of the bowels of his mind measurable shapes. It was not an act of creation because creation would produce the *real,* but the real had existed eternally. What Urizen produced was the finite appearance which obscures and conceals the infinite real. Or, rather, since "Earth was not, nor globes of attraction," he produced those *conceptions* of measurable shapes, which would later take physical form. Having these conceptions, he sees himself as a Creator-God and foresees that, out of the void over which he stretches self-balanced (but *self*-balance is a contradiction in terms—he is really falling like a one-winged bird), he will construct a universe. And so he will. The many, all his manifested diverse conceptions, will be turned into one, certainly, but only because they are compelled to it by

> One command, one joy, one desire,
> One curse, one weight, one measure,
> One King, one God, one Law.

His will be the unity of submissive obedience, not of collaborative equality.

The tragic irony of the situation is that Urizen, having separated from the One, seeks Oneness. What he fails to understand is that a *dynamic* unity is impossible without the interaction of contraries. Joy could not know itself without pain; an *unburning* desire or imagination is a contradiction in terms; an unfluctuating solid would be lifeless. The fact is that the greater the contrast between the contraries is, the more intense the consciousness is. But Urizen does not want intense consciousness; he wants the spiritual torpor of "holiness." For him, everything half-dead is holy.

It has got to be recognized that Urizen is not *bad,* as in *Paradise Lost* and the *Divine Comedy* Satan is. He is in Error. He is not, therefore, thrown out of Heaven to be punished in an eternal Hell. No one is punished, but all suffer. The other Eternals, horrified observers of Urizen's aberrant thought, and yet incapable—and undesirous—of a complete separation from him (their salvation, like his, is in their ultimate reunification), respond immediately to counteract his

27

error. But, of course, themselves out of equilibrium, their response is not benevolently omnipotent.

Put it this way: Reason, separated from Love and Imagination and thus self-restrictive, cannot be Wisdom— though, of course, he thinks himself to be. Love and Imagination, separated from Reason and thus unconfined, likewise cannot be themselves but will become excesses of themselves — say, Pity and Wrath. Love and Wisdom, working together, are like a sun, emitting warmth and light. Love separated from Wisdom emits only fire. And the myriads of Eternity send fires (but no light) against Urizen. It is an effort to rectify his errors, the error of self-consciousness leading to the error of self-omnipotence leading to the error of rule of others by brass-bound, written law instead of spiritual understanding. But the "seven deadly sins of the soul" enter into and distort their efforts.

Urizen, then, is not moved to return to Eternity but runs "raging To hide," and builds over himself a "petrific" roof, which, cooled by veins of blood, protects him from the fires. For him (Reason seeking relief from burning "love") it is a womb to retreat to. To the Reason-less Eternals it seems a human heart "struggling and beating." It is, in fact, a firming up, a solidifying of Urizen's intention to live alone, a firm resolution made firmer in order to withstand the anger of the passion and the imagination. That is, cosmologically, Urizen has fixed the outer bounds of the universe-to-be, within which are the as-yet chaotic (unorganized) seeds of all things animal, vegetable, and mineral.

Now, as was said, if Wisdom separating from Love becomes less than Wisdom — that is, becomes analytical reason — and Love becomes less than Love and can no longer act with total affirmation, total out-going-ness, then the latter must do "hateful" things, and in so doing must inevitably become hateful — restrictive and thus restricted.

So Los (Chapter III, st. 8) is sent to take his place at the side of Urizen in the Chaos. Urizen falls asleep, indeed, appears to be dead. Los, as much wounded by his separation from Urizen as the latter, is himself in a tormented stupor. But he is the creative, not

28

the passive, principle, and can heal his wound and escape his stupor, as Urizen cannot. And Los cannot accept the idea of Death, nor can he accept a continuing Chaos. He becomes aware that Urizen is not dead, that he teems with monstrous, deathly, ever-shifting ideas, and he begins to take constructive action.

Here is the basic paradox of the poem: that Love, not Reason, has to bring Order out of Chaos, and to do so has to invent Time, has to inflict Urizen's (and his own) mind with forgetfulness, dumbness, and necessity, and has to make Urizen manifest, giving him a skull, a spine, and skeletal structure, a heart and nervous system, eyes, ears, nose, and throat.[40] That is, where Urizen in Eternity had been part of the One Whole Man having infinite spiritual being in wisdom and joy of life, he now becomes a Partial Man in Time manifested through the void. He is not the Universe, though he extends through all the void. He is one of two principles, the other being Los, which together form, so to speak, a *Biverse*. Where, in Eternity, Los and Urizen, though contraries, had worked as a team, now, in Time, though still contraries, they pull in diverse directions.

His seven labors of manifestation completed, Los lapses into Urizen's dormant state; a nerveless silence, a cold solitude, a dark void closes in upon him. He has, one might say, incarnated Wisdom, confined it in a philosophical system. Love-Imagination is assimilated into that system, loses its fiery liveliness and its capability of inciting active, original thought. But from this sleep, impelled by the desire which is never altogether absent from the creative principle (Chapter V, st. 5), Los awakes. And he sees that the Biverse which has been formed, and of which he and Urizen are principles, is void, is without life. Perhaps it lacks the ether through which the warmth and light of wisdom and love can be transmitted. It is not, in any case, to be called Space, since Space, conceived as a receptacle, is void until it contains objects, or, conceived as an attribute of the objects, cannot exist without them.

---

40—It is to be noted that the sense of Touch is omitted. This, representing Sex, was less closely restricted than the others, offering the most immediate possibility of return to the Eternal.

Therefore, Los, still affirmative and loving, contemplates with pity the lonely, death-like state of Urizen. But his love is not *totally* affirmative and out-going; it is tainted with self-pity, a divisive emanation, effeminate and effeminizing, altogether absent when Love exists in its totality of affirmation. So, from the formerly androgynous Immortal, the separated feminine principle Enitharmon is born, introducing Sex and Generation. (Since the concept of Space implies *increase, infinite divisibility,* it can be inferred that Enitharmon symbolizes Space as well as Pity. In later poems she does; here Blake does not specify.)

The residents of Eternity are horrified by the sight of this new creature and, very soon, by the sight of Los and Enitharmon in the sexual embrace. And they begin the final separation of Time-Space from Eternity (Chapter V., st. 11) by limiting the perception of Urizen-Los-Enitharmon to the scientific observation of Time-Space. (When, after Sex, Generation eventually occurred and the child Orc was born, "no more Los beheld Eternity.") Things are now in a serious state of confusion. The Eternals have sent Los to heal or at least quarantine the ailing Urizen. But Los himself falls ill. So the remaining Eternals repudiate them both. The paradox consists in this, that isolation of any part militates against the restitution of the whole. And, of course, the isolation is commanded in the name of Science.

Already, because of the division into sexes, Los has experienced lust, cruelty, and perversity, and Enitharmon has in sorrow brought forth her child, who has himself undergone monstrous phylogenetic changes. Now Los succumbs to the frightful pangs of Jealousy, and, as though he were the tyrant Jupiter, chains his new-born child to a mountain.

Thus, to summarize the action to this point:

1. Wisdom, separating from Love in Eternity, became Reason in the Void.

2. Love, seeking to halt Reason's fall from grace, enters the Void and binds Reason in Time.

3. Reason falls into a deathly sleep, and Love undertakes his manifestation, limiting his powers of immediate and total perception.

4. In doing so, Love himself is limited and changed, Pity and Sex taking "concrete" form. Space joins Time to become the future habitation and condition of Nature. The Void, however, persists.

5. A Life Impulse (Orc) is born of the sexual union of Love and Pity, so that Urizen need no longer dwell in a Void "undivided by existence."

6. Love, the Life Principle in Eternity, and still so in Time-Space but with dwindling powers, like an aging tyrant jealously rejects his son.

Here a tremendous irony is realized. Los has placed Orc under the shadow of Urizen, apparently assuming that this will destroy or inhibit his (Orc's) powers. But the contrary occurs. All those ideas in Urizen's brain are agitated into lively motion—all those shapes

Of beast, bird, fish, serpent and element,
Combustion, blast, vapour and cloud.

And Urizen (Chapter VII, st. 6), exploring the terrain, measuring, weighing, manifesting the four elemental materials, forms Chaos (the Void) into Newton's Nature.

So Earth and all its inhabitants (Chapter VIII) are produced— but under the most inauspicious circumstances. In the first place, Los (after one last ambiguous action) withdraws from the scene. Neither he nor Enitharmon nor Orc plays any further *overt* part in the narrative. Second, all of Urizen's creations are under his (Urizen's) curse, since he has imposed upon them his "iron laws," laws quite impossible of being complied with. The condition of all life must therefore be sin and death.

Recognition of this awakens "Pity" (Chapter VIII, st. 6) in Urizen's heart (or mind). That is, he undergoes a spiritual perturbation analogous to that experienced by Los when he observed the fallen Urizen. But Urizen is now to such a degree removed from Los

31

that the pity he feels is only the palest, coldest shadow of that felt by Los. Enitharmon, after all, though divided from Love, at least affirmed Sexual Generation and produced the Promethean Orc. But the "pity" of Urizen is born as Restrictive Religion.

That is to say that all Nature shrinks into finiteness. All of Urizen's sons and daughters—elements, vegetables, animals, man— had been at their inception (however monstrous from the point of view of unmanifested Eternity) *eternal* sons and daughters. Now in the six days described in *Genesis* (falsely described as the days of creation; they are really days of restriction of perception) they forget their eternal life. Since Man sees only the Newtonian universe, only that universe exists. (For natural objects, the rule is: I am seen by man; therefore I exist. From which follows the corollary: I exist in the way that I am seen.)

Nevertheless, though the field is lost, all is not lost. In that ambiguous action in Chapter VII,

> But Los encircled Enitharmon
> With Fires of Prophecy
> From the sight of Urizen and Orc
> And she bore an enormous race,

Los does a selfish thing: he takes true Pity to himself, leaving Enlivened Reason only Hypocritical Pity. So, as Blake later reveals, the blame for what Urizen does can be ascribed to Los:

> Thus the terrible race of Los and Enitharmon gave
> Laws and Religions to the sons of Har, binding them more
> And more to Earth, closing and restraining,
> Till a Philosophy of Five Senses was complete.
> Urizen wept & gave it into the hands of Newton and
> Locke. [41]

Yet, though Los and Enitharmon have "mortalized" Man, they are also, behind those "fires of Prophecy," making possible his salvation. Or at least Blake will take this position when he comes to write *The Four Zoas:*

---

41—*The Song of Los.*

32

Enitharmon wove in tears, singing songs of Lamentations
And pitying comfort as she sigh'd forth on the wind the
    spectres
And wove them bodies, calling them her belov'd sons &
    daughters,
Employing the daughters in her looms, & Los employ'd
    the sons
In Golgonooza's Furnaces among the Anvils of time &
    space,
Thus forming a vast family, wondrous in beauty & love,
And they appear'd a Universal female form created
From those who were dead in Ulro, from the spectres of
    the dead. [42]

In the present poem, nothing about what Los and Enitharmon do behind the fires is made explicit. However, Orc, who had enlivened Urizen and Nature, though still chained and no longer mentioned by Blake, must be assumed to continue in his enlivening power. At any rate, Fuzon, the element of fire, gathers together such children of Urizen as are not altogether "wither'd and deafen'd and cold," and conducts an exodus from the earth in order to attempt an overthrow of Urizen's dictatorship. He fails (in the succeeding *Book of Ahania*) and is nailed to the Tree of Mystery. Even so, his "fiery beam" was to the wandering, lost tribes of Earth a pillar of fire for five hundred years, when Los, heating it "in a mass/With the body of the sun," turned it into sunlight.

Thus Blake's earliest attempt at cosmogony. To carry on the outline on page 30:

    7. The son of Love and Pity, a Life Impulse, awakens Urizen, who is moved to "create" Nature in the Void.

    8. Sin and death afflict Nature, and Urizen generates Restrictive Religion, which gives a delusive hope that through abnegation of natural powers they (sin and death) may be overcome.

    9. But Fuzon—of a kind with Los and Orc (and Jesus)—gives a hint of salvationary things to come

---

42—*The Four Zoas*, Night 8.

by rebelling against the tyranny of dogmatic religion.

It seems unquestionable that the *Book of Urizen* was intended as a counteraction of the "false" view of God and the creation promulgated by Milton. The differences between Blake's and Milton's accounts are profound: In Milton, God is sole and transcendent Lord of all, omnipotent, benevolent, and unchanging. In Milton, it is not God who falls but angelic beings created by Him and separate from Him, and the cosmic creation consequent upon the fall of these beings is benevolently purposed by omnipotence. In Milton, all good is on one side and all evil on the other. In Milton, the virtues tend to be obedience and rational self-control.

In brief, Blake's is a far more subtle, complex, and *scientific* account than Milton's. It is so because it is a cosmogony based upon a psychology which is strikingly modern. As W. P. Witcutt says:

> The great value of Blake's poetry is that it provides a kind of outline of the unconscious mind. Blake explored this strange region more thoroughly than any before or since, and what is more, he knew what he was doing.
>
>                    "I rest not from my great task
> To open the Eternal Worlds, to open the immortal Eyes
> Of Man inwards into the World of Thought, into Eternity."
>
> And the point is that the things he discovered in the inner world, the godlike figures and the symbols, were not peculiar to himself. They are to be found—altered only in inessentials—in the inner world of every man. For that world is for each of us the same. In exploring the mythological world of Blake we are really exploring our own minds. [43]

To demonstrate this, let us read the poem as the history of a child's development instead of a universe's. As a child William Blake enjoyed that unity of the mind which resides in a biological co-ordination of its differentiated aspects. His Ego took its proper place as the centrum of his field of consciousness, no more than a complex among complexes; it had not, disallowing the function of the unconscious psyche, defined itself as the soul, the total Self, or even as the *good*

---

43—W. P. Witcutt, *Blake, A Psychological Study,* p. 18.

part of the Self, the only part not subject to mortality and therefore the law-giving part. The young Blake did not agree with Descartes that "it is certain that I am really distinct from my body and can exist without it." Un-obsessed by Sex, he took delight in the pleasurable activity of all parts of the body, with no special (or prurient) focus upon the genital; unaware of the Anima as such, he did not find evil and accordingly deny the feminine qualities rising out of his unconscious; unconcerned about such pragmatically-contrived abstractions as Chastity, Latent Homosexuality, Sin, and the Future of the Race, he felt no guilt in naked physical contact nor any practical interest in Generation, but, with his playfellows, sweetly roamed from field to field and washed in a river and shone in the sun. He had not arrived at "the European and Western ideal of the self-aware individual confronting destiny with his own indomitable will and skeptical reason as the only factors on which he can rely." [44] (Nor had it become evident to him, though it was later to do so, that "this ideal was a moral mistake and an intellectual error, for it exaggerated the ethical, philosophical, and scientific importance of the awareness of the individual.") [45]

In short, he lived in Innocence, which is Eternity—until his personal *Book of Urizen* began.

(1 and 2) [46] For at some point, perhaps at age fourteen, [47] the

44—Lancelot Law Whyte, *The Unconscious before Freud,* p. 6.
45—*Ibid.*
46—These numbers correspond with those on pages 30 and 33 detailing the cosmological changes that occur in the poem.
47—But perhaps earlier. It was at age seven that Edwin Muir (see *An Autobiography,* pp. 33-5) lost the vision of innocence, which he describes as follows:
And a child has also a picture of human existence peculiar to himself, which he probably never remembers after he has lost it: the original vision of the world. I think of this picture or vision as that of a state in which the earth, the houses on the earth, and the life of every human being are related to the sky overarching them; as if the sky fitted the earth and the earth the sky. Certain dreams convince me that a child has this vision, in which there is a completer harmony of all things with each other than he will ever know again. There comes a moment (the moment at which childhood passes into boyhood or girlhood) when this image is broken and contradiction enters life. It is a phase of emotional and mental strain, and it brings with it a sense of guilt.

condition of his life underwent a shocking change. It would appear that he experienced what Jung calls a "psychic catastrophe," that is, that his transition from childhood to adolescence was less evolutionary than revolutionary and that some specific and unforgettable traumatic event marked the transition. What this event might have been Blake was never to reveal, unless he did so under the cover of symbolic distortion in the following passage in *Jerusalem* from which Witcutt infers a reason-confounding "narcissistic delight in the beauty of his own body" which caused his personality to disintegrate:

> We reared mighty Stones, we danced naked around them,
> Thinking to bring Love into light of day, to Jerusalem's shame
> Displaying our Giant limbs to all the winds of heaven. Sudden
> Shame seiz'd us, we could not look on one another for abhorrence. . . . [48]

In Jungian terms, the *ego* (the center of consciousness) was assimilated by the *self* (the totality of the psyche). In Blake's terms, Urizen falls under the control of Los. Jung explains what follows from such an occurrence:

> The image of wholeness then remains in the unconscious, so that on the one hand it shares the archaic nature of the unconscious and on the other hand finds itself in the psychically relative space-time continuum that is characteristic of the unconscious as such. Both these qualities are numinous and hence have an unlimited determining effect on ego-consciousness, which is differentiated, *i.e.,* separated, from the unconscious and moreover exists in an absolute space and an absolute time. It is a vital necessity that this should be so. If, therefore, the ego falls for any length of time under the control of an unconscious factor, its adaptation is disturbed and the way opened for all sorts of possible accidents. [49]

---

48—*Op. cit.,* p. 57.

49—Violet S. de Laszlo, editor of *Psyche and Symbol, a Selection from the Writings of C. G. Jung,* 1958, p. 23.

The remedy is to anchor the ego in the world of consciousness and reinforce the consciousness by a very precise adaptation.

In the present poem, however, it is an element of the conscious mind rather than of the unconscious which initiates the offensive action: Urizen assumes a self-sufficiency which mobilizes the Eternals to a defensive response. In Jung's terms, ". . . accentuation of the ego personality and the world of consciousness may easily assume such proportions that the figures of the unconscious are *psychologized and the self consequenty becomes assimilated to the ego.*" What is required to restore some kind of balance is that "the world of consciousness be levelled down in favor of the reality of the unconscious."

Perhaps Blake did a calculatedly mean and selfish thing — for which he felt an exaggerated remorse—but which he rationalized and justified—but for which he continued to feel a guilt which he could never altogether repress. Or possibly a calculatedly mean thing was done him, perhaps by the brother he did not like or by the girl who departed (holy and meek) when he sought to tell his love—for which coldly reasonable act he first felt self-pity, jealousy, and wrath and then devised methods of retaliation which, even as he devised them, he felt to be shameful. Or perhaps he felt and rationalized and acted upon (symbolically rather than actually) a murderous rebelliousness against some "rational" social stricture and its human agent. There is, for example, the experience of the child in "Infant Sorrow":

And I sooth'd day after day
Till upon the ground I stray;
And I smil'd night after night,
Seeking only for delight.

And I saw before me shine
Clusters of the wand'ring vine,
And many a lovely flower & tree
Stretch'd their blossoms out to me.

My father then with holy look,
In his hands a holy book,
Pronounc'd curses on my head
And bound me in a mirtle shade.

In the succeeding poem ("In a Mirtle Shade"), the father laughs at the Blake who maintains that "Love, free love cannot be bound," and Blake reacts with significant violence:

So I smote him and his gore
Stained the roots my mirtle bore.

It was sacramental murder and therefore justifiable; it was murder nevertheless (Oresteian and most foul) and therefore soul-shaking. Nor would the psychoanalyst overlook the possibility that Blake is unconsciously striking at himself out of his frustration and disillusion as the creator of a false image of his father, which, without self-diminishment, he cannot modify to fit the facts.

According to the first assumption (Witcutt's, p. 36), Blake tries to conceal the true cause of the beginning of his disintegration—Passion assuming the prerogatives of Reason, the unconscious overpowering the conscious, libido compelling the ego to unnatural action. He does so by making Passion the *secondary* cause instead of the primary. The analyst might very well regard this distortion of the fact as being analogous to a characteristic dream-mechanism.

In the second assumption (Blake's doing a selfish thing), Blake does not *conceal* the true cause; he is merely *mistaken* in ascribing to his conscious mind a selfish act whose real source is the unconscious. (When he comes to write his later poems, he corrects that mistaken ascription.) According to the third, he reacted to calculated meanness in kind, but then, coming to recognize his reaction as egregious and self-annihilating, was able to answer the Smile of Deceit with the Smile of Love. Nevertheless, what Jung describes as "the resistance of the conscious mind to the unconscious and the depreciation of the latter" has not been altogether mitigated: the peace between the two is really a cold war. According to the fourth, his righteous reaction against the reasoned restrictions of the outside world was self-isolating, self-wounding, might even have come to be thought by him excessively self-righteous. Adjustments of the relations between the conscious and the unconscious were absolutely necessary.

(3). Whatever and whenever the traumatic event and whatever the immediate cause, Blake's essential unitary Innocence—a state of wise loving—is destroyed. Conscious and unconscious are set at odds. This occurring, the conscious begins to perceive life in terms of the reality-principle instead of the pleasure-principle. It learns to think in terms of *ought* instead of *is*. It limits and negates and represses, becomes obsessed with sin and the consequences of sin. It sows the sands of abstinence all over Blake's ruddy limbs and flaming hair, leaving desire ungratified. Blake's instinctive wisdom, the power of his mind to concur equally and immediately (without ratiocination) with his body's desires, lies dormant.

(4) That is, an unreflecting Love, neither selfish nor unselfish but merely seeking an outlet, is changed to self-concerned, cost-counting, law-fearing, cerebro-genital Sex. Awareness of the body as being distinct from the soul, and as having evil appetites that must be contained, is manifested. The young Blake becomes firmly fixed in the Space-Time of Maturity's sense of responsibility, and his vision of life is determined by the categories of Good and Evil. Himself impoverished, he has but little love to bestow on others. Since love has become sex and sex is evil, he cannot engage in a marriage of true minds *and* bodies. What is left him to confer is at best that awkward, uncertain and therefore brusque (even, sometimes, cruel) but essentially sympathetic amiability that is characteristic of adolescents suffering from "anxious desire." He has been compelled to make someone poor; if he cannot love, he can pity. But not with assurance, since he does not know what he is doing, nor what he has been restrained from doing, nor why. He is a citizen of a chaos, not of the world. And, further, his pity is as much ingrowing as outgoing. An affirming, creative love is to such a degree diminished into self-love and self-pity that an "infinite labour" of rationalization is required to make the situation supportable.

(5) However, The Puer Aeternus, the "inner man," the divine spark, refuses to be extinguished. It asserts itself—perhaps in an impulse toward art and poetry.

(6) But this assertion is at once inhibited. Shades of the prison-house continue to close round the growing boy; the reality-principle

subjugates the pleasure-principle; the super-ego quells the libido; the individual gives in to the rationalizations of society; the death wish erodes the life-drive. Schizophrenia is imminent.

(7) Nevertheless, this rebellious Impulsiveness, never saying die, so acts that the death-wish cannot triumph. It forces the consciousness to create a world that is endurable. Not at all a satisfactory world, restricted and methodized as it is, but at least one in which life and pleasure are not altogether denied.

(8) Even the consciousness, however it represses the desires and impulses of the unconscious, realizes that it has created a sad world, made so by the awareness of sin and death, and it strives for some means of palliation. But, as always, negative, distrustful of the body and its passions and instincts, the consciousness postulates itself as the total life-principle and offers as the only hope of eternal life continued repression of the unconscious.

(9) But the fiery impulses of the unconscious refuse to be damped and break out into a new form. They fuse into one, and, against all odds, traverse their waste land seeking the land of milk and honey.

———  ———  ———  ———

This account is neither Freudian nor Jungian but a kind of mish-mash. It is also an extreme simplification as compared to what a trained psychologist would present. Though it has often been said that all of Freud's teachings are to be found in Blake, the latter's relation to Jung seems even closer. An article in *TLS* (2 Aug., '63) characterizing Jung as of an introverted, schizoid disposition might, as a few quotations will show, have been written as a description of Blake:

> In compensation for his lack of adaption to the external world the boy discovered or imagined within himself a person who was "important, a high authority, a man not to be trifled with: who was in a special personal relationship with God, who seemed to speak both directly and in dreams. . . ."

———  ———  ———

40

The private revelations which emanated from this deity were by no means conventional. Strange phallic images and a vision of the Almighty obscenely destroying his own cathedral were secrets which could not be shared with others, and which drove Jung further in upon himself to become increasingly convinced both that he had been granted a special insight, and also that he would be inevitably misunderstood.

— — — —

It is a commonplace of psychiatry that schizophrenics tend to personify their mental contents, so that ideas and feelings which originate from within their own minds appear to them as the "voices" of other persons. Jungian psychology is full of such personifications. Shadow, anima and other archetypal figures are but names given by Jung to contents of his own mind which seemed alien to his unconscious ego.

— — — —

Such persons suffer from deep divisions within the mind, and, in the more acute varieties of this disorder, often believe themselves to be a battleground of good and evil forces. Jung demonstrated, both in his life and in his writing, that some kind of reconciliation between such opposites is possible, even if it requires an esoteric religion to achieve this.

Schizophrenia is not by any means an exclusively modern condition. What is modern [50] is the "discovery" of, and the methodized study of, and the high value placed upon the unconscious as opposed to the conscious mind. Not Milton nor Locke nor the high priests of the Enlightenment would have written as Lancelot Law Whyte wrote in 1960:

> . . . without a balanced conception of the unconscious it is hard to see how human dignity can be restored. For today, *faith, if it has any relation to the natural world, implies faith in the unconscious.* If there is a God he must speak there; if there is a healing power, it must operate there; if there is a principle of ordering in the organic realm, its most pow-

---

50—By modern I mean post-Freud as opposed to post-Locke.

erful manifestation must be found there. The unconscious mind is the expression of the organic in the individual.[51]

Since no English poet between Milton and Blake evinced so great a faith in "a balanced conception of the unconscious" or explored it so fully and expressed his discoveries so precisely, since none avowed so little faith in organizational Christianity, Lockean psychology, Newtonian cosmology, or Cartesian dualism, Blake stands as the first modern poet, his intellectual leap beyond Milton being so great as to be not a development but a mutation. His prophetic poems are, I repeat, not so much theological or philosophical as scientific.

☆    ☆    ☆

*The Book of Urizen* ends with its hero—Man seen by expanded vision, Blake seen by contracted vision—and his universe still out of kilter. It would be a pity not to show paradise regained. Here are excerpts from *Milton, The Four Zoas,* and *Jerusalem* showing God (Man) and Sinner (Man) reconciled. First, Milton speaks to explain the true way to salvation:

But turning toward Ololon in terrible majesty Milton
Replied: "Obey thou the Words of the Inspired Man.
"All that can be annihilated must be annihilated
"That the Children of Jerusalem may be saved from slavery.
"There is a Negation, & there is a Contrary:
"The Negation must be destroy'd to redeem the Contraries.
"The Negation is the Spectre, the Reasoning Power in Man:
"This is a false Body, an Incrustation over my Immortal
"Spirit, a Selfhood which must be put off & annihilated
    alway.
"To cleanse the Face of my Spirit by Self-examination,
"To bathe in the Waters of Life, to wash off the Not
    Human,
  "I come in Self-annihilation & the grandeur of Inspiration,
  "To cast off Rational Demonstration by Faith in the Saviour,

---

51—*Op. cit.,* p. 7.

"To cast off the rotten rags of Memory by Inspiration,
"To cast off Bacon, Locke & Newton from Albion's
    covering,
"To take off his filthy garments & clothe him with
    Imagination,
"To cast aside from Poetry all that is not Inspiration,
"That it no longer shall dare to mock with the aspersion
    of Madness
"Cast on the Inspired by the tame high finisher of paltry
    Blots
"Indefinite, or paltry Rhymes, or paltry Harmonies,
"Who creeps into State Government like a catterpiller to
    destroy;
"To cast off the idiot Questioner who is always questioning
"But never capable of answering, who sits with a sly grin
"Silent plotting when to question, like a thief in a cave,
"Who publishes doubt & calls it knowledge, whose Science
    is Despair,
"Whose pretence to knowledge is Envy, whose whole
    Science is
"To destroy the wisdom of ages to gratify ravenous Envy
"That rages round him like a Wolf day & night without
    rest:
"He smiles with condescension, he talks of Benevolence
    & Virtue,
"And those who act with Benevolence & Virtue they murder
    time on time.
"These are the destroyers of Jerusalem, these are the
    murderers
"Of Jesus, who deny the Faith & mock at Eternal Life,
"Who pretend to Poetry that they may destroy Imagination
"By imitation of Nature's Images drawn from Remembrance.
"These are the Sexual Garments, the Abomination of
    Desolation,
"Hiding the Human Lineaments as with an Ark & Curtains
"Which Jesus rent & now shall wholly purge away with Fire
"Till Generation is swallow'd up in Regeneration."

In *The Four Zoas* Blake describes the beneficent results of self-annihilation in relatively general terms:

> The Sun has left his blackness & has found a fresher morning,
> And the mild moon rejoices in the clear & cloudless night,
> And Man walks forth from midst of the fires: the evil is all consum'd.
> His eyes behold the Angelic spheres arising night & day;
> The stars consum'd like a lamp blown out, & in their stead, behold
> The Expanding Eyes of Man behold the depths of wondrous worlds!
> One Earth, one sea beneath; nor Erring Globes wander, but Stars
> Of fire rise up nightly from the Ocean; & one Sun
> Each morning, like a New born Man, issues with songs & joy
> Calling the Plowman to his Labour & the Shepherd to his rest.
> He walks upon the Eternal Mountains, raising his heavenly voice,
> Conversing with the Animal forms of wisdom night & day,
> That, risen from the Sea of fire, renew'd walk o'er the Earth;
> For Tharmas brought his flocks upon the hills, & in the Vales
> Around the Eternal Man's bright tent, the little Children play
> Among the wooly flocks. The hammer of Urthona sounds
> In the deep caves beneath; his limbs renew'd, his Lions roar
> Around the Furnaces & in Evening sport upon the plains.
> They raise their faces from the Earth, conversing with the Man:
> "How is it we have walk'd thro' fires & yet are not consum'd?
> "How is it that all things are chang'd, even as in ancient times?"

The Sun arises from his dewy bed, & the fresh airs
Play in his smiling beams giving the seeds of life to grow,
And the fresh Earth beams forth ten thousand thousand
  springs of life.
Urthona is arisen in his strength, no longer now
Divided from Enitharmon, no longer the Spectre Los.
Where is the Spectre of Prophecy? where is the delusive
  Phantom?
Departed: & Urthona rises from the ruinous Walls
In all his ancient strength to form the golden armour of
  science
For intellectual War. The war of swords departed now,
The dark Religions are departed & sweet Science reigns.

But in *Jerusalem* this pastoral sketch is elaborated into a triumphal pageant in which both the contracted and the expanded vision are brought into play. The four Zoas *and* England are depicted in concomitant regeneration. For when "The Breath Divine went forth over the morning hills," England, indeed the British Empire, discovered humanity, whereupon nationalism and imperialism were, like Milton's self-hood and Urizen's solipsism, purged away:

The Four Living Creatures, Chariots of Humanity Divine
  Incomprehensible,
In beautiful Paradises expand. These are the Four Rivers of
  Paradise
And the Four Faces of Humanity, fronting the Four
  Cardinal Points
Of Heaven, going forward, forward irresistible from
  Eternity to Eternity.
And they conversed together in Visionary forms dramatic
  which bright
Redounded from their Tongues in thunderous majesty, in
  Visions
In new Expanses, creating exemplars of Memory and of
  Intellect,

Creating Space, Creating Time, according to the wonders Divine

Of Human Imagination throughout all the Three Regions immense

Of Childhood, Manhood & Old Age; & the all tremendous unfathomable Non Ens

Of Death was seen in regenerations terrific or complacent, varying

According to the subject of discourse; & every Word & every Character

Was Human according to the Expansion or Contraction, the Translucence or

Opakeness of Nervous fibres: such was the variation of Time & Space

Which vary according as the Organs of Perception vary; & they walked

To & fro in Eternity as One Man, reflecting each in each & clearly seen

And seeing, according to fitness & order. And I heard Jehovah speak

Terrific from his Holy Place, & saw the Words of the Mutual Covenant Divine

On Chariots of gold & jewels, with Living Creatures, starry & flaming

With every Colour, Lion, Tyger, Horse, Elephant, Eagle, Dove, Fly, Worm

And the all wondrous Serpent clothed in gems & rich array, Humanize

In the Forgiveness of Sins according to thy Covenant, Jehovah. They Cry:

"Where is the Covenant of Priam, the Moral Virtues of the Heathen?

"Where is the Tree of Good & Evil that rooted beneath the cruel heel

"Of Albions Spectre, the Patriarch Druid? where are all his Human Sacrifice

"For Sin in War & in the Druid Temples of the Accuser of Sin, beneath

46

"The Oak Groves of Albion that cover'd the whole Earth
  beneath his Spectre?
"Where are the Kingdoms of the World & all their glory
  that grew on Desolation,
"The Fruit of Albion's Poverty Tree, when the Triple
  Headed Gog-Magog Giant
"Of Albion Taxed the Nations into Desolation & then gave
  the Spectrous Oath?"
Such is the Cry from all the Earth, from the Living Creatures
  of the Earth
And from the great City of Golgonooza in the Shadowy
  Generation,
And from the Thirty-two Nations of the Earth among the
  Living Creatures.
All Human Forms identified, even Tree, Metal, Earth &
  Stone: all
Human Forms identified, living, going forth & returning
  wearied
Into the Planetary lives of Years, Months, Days & Hours;
  reposing,
And then Awaking into his Bosom in the Life of Immor-
  tality.
And I heard the Name of their Emanations: they are named
  Jerusalem.

One must ask whether anything in the English poetry of triumph
(save possibly *Prometheus Unbound's* last act) approaches this either
in magnitude of conception or grandeur of expression. "Surely," says
Longinus, "great words are spoken only by those who think great
thoughts." But often enough the words of great souls are greatest
when they describe catastrophe, not triumph. Even Homer, Longinus
notes, has been guilty of giving eternity "not to the *being* of the
gods but to their *misfortunes.*" Had Longinus read Milton he might
have said no less. It does not seem an untenable conclusion that, so
far as the Western world is concerned, only in the *Paradiso,* and in
certain Italian paintings, Gothic cathedrals, and German musical com-
positions, does a parallel exist with Blake's concluding jubilation.

The importance of the *Book of Urizen* is that here Blake
planted the acorn from which *Jerusalem's* oak emerged.

47

# Illustrations

The following pages present photographic reproductions of the Trianon Press facsimile of an original *Book of Urizen* owned by Mr. Lessing J. Rosenwald. Some originals contain 28 plates. The Rosenwald original, lacking Plate 4, contains only twenty seven. Without Plate 4, forty lines of the poem (from "Muster around the black desarts" in Chapter II to "All the deadly sins of the soul" in Chapter III) are missing. However, the Trianon Press facsimile is so superior to the one annotated by Dorothy Plowman that there was no question which should be reproduced.

Blake did not maintain a given order of illustrations in the seven copies of the book which he issued. Thus, some difficulty attaches to associating the illustrations with the events of the poem. Damon defends Blake's practice on the ground that the "states" being represented are eternal, happening everywhere at all times, and therefore must not be conceived as having a single, correct chronological order. Nevertheless, he "rearranges the plates . . . so that they tell their story as clearly as possible."

The plates in the Rosenwald copy do not accord with Damon's rearrangement. Their order is as follows:

Plate 1. Title page. Urizen under the Tree of Mystery (see *Ahania*, Chapter II) writing his "secrets of wisdom . . . secrets of dark contemplation" (Chapter II, *Book of Urizen*).

Plate 2. *Preludium.* According to Damon, Enitharmon floating in Space with Orc; according to Dorothy Plowman, the soul of a Babe in Eternity being invited by Nature to enter Time. Perhaps it is a word sent by the Eternals to William Blake.

Plate 3. According to Damon, Los afire with inspiration; according to Dorothy Plowman, Urizen fighting "with the fire consum'd Inwards" (Chapter II). If Plowman is right, this would seem to be the Urizen who sought "a joy without pain," and objected to living in "unquenchable burnings" (Chapter II).

Plate 4. Urizen under his petrific roof (Chapter I, and Chapter III).

Plate 5. Urizen displaying his book of eternal brass (Chapter II).

Plate 6. Urizen in his "ocean of voidness unfathomable" (Chapter III).

Plate ⸌7. Three Eternals, seized with rage, fall in "cataracts of fire, blood, & gall," wrapped around by the "seven deadly sins of the soul" (Chapter III).

Plate 8. The "self balanc'd" Urizen of Chapter II.

Plate 9. Los, "Groaning! gnashing! groaning!" (Chapter III).

Plate 10. Urizen, his nerves of joy frozen over by bones of solidness (Chapter IVb).

Plate 11. Urizen, chained, weeping, haloed with self-righteousness, presumably because "he wept & he called it Pity" (Chapter VIII).

Plate 12. According to Damon, Los "trying to rise in the petrific darkness." But perhaps stony sleep (Chapter IVb) settling down on Urizen.

Plate 13. Urizen and Los in a mutual "state of dismal woe" (Chapter IVb); Los perhaps shrinking (Chapter V) in terrors from his task.

Plate 14. A compressed, sorrowing Los, perhaps described in Chapter V: "Los wept obscur'd with mourning, / His bosom earthquak'd with sighs" or in Chapter III: "And a fathomless void for his feet / And intense fires for his dwelling."

Plate 15. According to Damon, Urizen's emanation, Ahania (see ll. 38-43 in *The Book of Ahania*). But possibly a representation of pity dividing Los's soul (Chapter V).

Plate 16. The expanding eyes of the Immortals behold the dark visions of Los and begin to weave curtains of darkness (Chapter V).

Plate 17. Enitharmon divides from Los, a globe of life blood branching out into roots (Chapter V).

Plate 18. Los, in the world of matter, but a virile figure with powerful positive capabilities. Perhaps complementary to Plate 8, the most positive representation of Urizen.

Plate 19. Enitharmon waving before the face of Los, curtains of darkness beginning to separate them from the Eternals (Chapter V).

Plate 20. Orc issuing with fierce flames (Chapter VI).

Plate 21. The Holy Family — Enitharmon, Orc, and Los, the last now constricted by chains of jealousy and, like Urizen, bearded (Chapter VII).

Plate 22. Urizen exploring his dens (Chapter VIII).

Plate 23. Urizen wandering upon the aged heavens, the "living Mantle adjoined to his life & growing from his Soul" (see *The Four Zoas,* Chapter VI) extended behind him, soon to turn into the Net of Religion (Chapter VIII).

Plate 24. The birth of the four elements (Chapter VIII).

Plate 25. The birth of Urizen's daughters from "monsters and worms of the pit" (Chapter VIII).

Plate 26. The "Dog at the wintry door" (Chapter VIII) that evokes Urizen's "pity," which is ironically contrasted with that of the boy who prays in the integrity of his innocence.

Plate 27. Urizen impotent, hearing the howl of the dog and the prayer of the boy and incapable, by himself, of mitigating their anguish.

# Literature Cited

Anon., "Two Faces of Jung," *TLS* (2 August, 1963).

Blake, William, *The Book of Urizen* (reproduced in facsimile, with a note by Dorothy Plowman), London and New York, 1929.

Blake, William, *Poetry and Prose,* ed. Geoffrey Keynes, The Nonesuch Press, Bloomsbury, 1932.

Blake, William, *Poetry and Prose,* ed. David V. Erdman, commentary by Harold Bloom, New York, 1965.

Blake, William, *Prophetic Writings,* ed. D. J. Sloss and J. P. R. Wallis, Oxford, 1925 (2 vols.).

Bloom, Harold, *Blake's Apocalypse,* Garden City, 1963.

Boehme, Jacob, *The Way to Christ,* trans. by John Joseph Stoudt, New York, 1947.

Damon, S. Foster, *William Blake: His Philosophy and Symbols,* New York, 1947.

de Laszlo, Violet S. ed., *Psyche and Symbol, a Selection from the Writings of G. G. Jung,* Garden City, 1958.

d'Olivet, Fabre, trans. *Cain* by Lord Byron, New York and London, 1923.

Grant, Robert McQueen, *Gnosticism, a Source Book of Heretical Writings from the Early Christian Period,* New York, 1961.

Guitton, Jean, *Great Heresies and Church Councils,* trans. by F. D. Wieck, New York, 1965.

Harper, George Mills, *The Neoplatonism of William Blake,* Chapel Hill, 1961.

Hirsch, E. D., *Innocence and Experience, an Introduction to Blake,* New Haven, 1964.

Hobhouse, Stephen, ed. *Sacred and Mystical Writings of William Law,* New York, 1948.

Huxley, Aldous, *The Perennial Philosophy,* London, 1946.

Jonas, Hans, *The Gnostic Religion,* Boston, 1963.

Kingsland, William, *The Gnosis or Ancient Wisdom in the Christian Scriptures,* London, 1954.

Muir, Edwin, *An Autobiography,* New York, 1954.

Percival, M. O., *William Blake's Circle of Destiny,* New York, 1938.

Pound, Ezra, "The New Age" (11 February, 1915), p. 409.

Raine, Kathleen, "Blake's Debt to Antiquity," *Sewanee Review,* 71 (Summer, 1963), 352-451.

Saurat, Denis, *Literature and Occult Tradition,* New York, 1930.

Schorer, Mark, *William Blake: The Politics of Vision,* New York, 1946.

Symons, Arthur, *William Blake,* London, 1907.

Whyte, Lancelot Law, *The Unconscious Before Freud,* New York, 1962.

Witcutt, W. P., *Blake, A Psychological Study,* London, 1946.

THE
BOOK
of
URIZEN

LAMBETH. Printed by W.ᵐ Blake 1794

PRELUDIUM

TO

THE

BOOK OF

URIZEN

Of the primeval Priests assum'd power,
When Eternals spurn'd back his religion;
And gave him a place in the north,
Obscure, shadowy, void, solitary.

Eternals I hear your call gladly,
Dictate swift winged words, & fear not
To unfold your dark visions of torment.

2

## Chap: I

1. Lo, a shadow of horror is risen
In Eternity! Unknown, unprolific!
Self-clos'd, all-repelling: what Demon
Hath form'd this abominable void
This soul-shudd'ring vacuum? — Some said
"It is Urizen", But unknown, abstracted
Brooding secret, the dark power hid.

2. Times on times he divided, & measur'd
Space by space in his ninefold darkness
Unseen, unknown! changes appear'd
In his desolate mountains rifted furious
By the black winds of perturbation

3. For he strove in battles dire
In unseen conflictions with shapes
Bred from his forsaken wilderness,
Of beast, bird, fish, serpent & element
Combustion, blast, vapour and cloud.

4. Dark revolving in silent activity:
Unseen in tormenting passions;
An activity unknown and horrible;
A self-contemplating shadow,
In enormous labours occupied

5. But Eternals beheld his vast forests
Age on ages he lay, clos'd, unknown
Brooding shut in the deep, all avoid
The petrific abominable chaos

6. His cold horrors silent, dark Urizen
Prepar'd: his ten thousands of thunders
Rang'd in gloom'd array stretch out across
The dread world, & the rolling of wheels
As of swelling seas, sound in his clouds
In his hills of stor'd snows, in his mountains
Of hail & ice; voices of terror,
Are heard, like thunders of autumn
When the cloud blazes over the harvests

## Chap: II

1. Earth was not: nor globes of attraction
The will of the Immortal expanded
Or contracted his all flexible senses.
Death was not, but eternal life sprung

2. The sound of a trumpet the heavens
Awoke & vast clouds of blood roll'd
Round the dim rocks of Urizen, so nam'd
That solitary one in Immensity

Shrill the trumpet: & myriads of Eternity,

In living creations appear'd
In the flames of eternal fury.

3. Sundring, dark'ning, thund'ring:
Rent away with a terrible crash
Eternity rolld wide apart
Wide asunder rolling
Mountainous all around
Departing; departing; departing;
Leaving ruinous fragments of life
Hanging frowning cliffs & all between
An ocean of voidness unfathomable.

4. The roaring fires ran o'er the heavns
In whirlwinds & cataracts of blood
And o'er the dark deserts of Urizen
Fires pour thro the void on all sides
On Urizens self-begotten armies.

5. But no light from the fires, all was
            darkness
In the flames of Eternal fury

6. In fierce anguish & quenchless
            flames

To the deserts and rocks he ran ra
To hide, but he could not: combining
He dug mountains & hills in vast strength,
He piled them in incessant labour,
In howlings & pangs & fierce madness
Long periods in burning fires labouring
Till hoary, and age-broke, and aged,
In despair and the shadows of death.

7. And a roof vast petrific around,
On all sides he framd: like a womb;
Where thousands of rivers in veins
Of blood pour down the mountains to cool
The eternal fires beating without
From Eternals; & like a black globe
View'd by sons of Eternity, standing
On the shore of the infinite ocean
Like a human heart strugling & beating
The vast world of Urizen appear'd.

8. And Los round the dark globe of
            Urizen,
Kept watch for Eternals to confine,
The obscure separation alone;
For Eternity stood wide apart,

Urizen Ch: III.

As the stars are apart from the earth  10. But Urizen laid in a stony sleep
9. Los wept howling around the dark  Unorganiz'd rent from Eternity
  Demon:
And cursing his lot for in anguish:
Urizen was rent from his side;  11. The Eternals said: What is this? Death
& a fathomless void for his feet:  Urizen is a clod of clay.
& intense fires for his dwelling

12: Los howld in a dismal stupor,
Groaning! gnashing! groaning,
Till the wrenching apart was healed

13: But the wrenching of Urizen
heald not
Cold featureless, flesh or clay

Rifted with direful changes,
He lay in a dreamless night

14: Till Los rouzd his fires
affrighted
At the formless unmeasurable
death.

Chap: IV:

1: Los smitten with astonish-ment
Frightend at the hurtling bones

2: And at the surging sulphure-ous
Perturbed Immortal mad raging

3: In whirlwinds & pitch & nitre
Round the furious limbs of Los

4: And Los formed nets & gins
And threw the nets round about

5: He watch'd in shuddring fear
The dark changes & bound every change
With rivets of iron & brass;

6. And these were the changes of Urizen

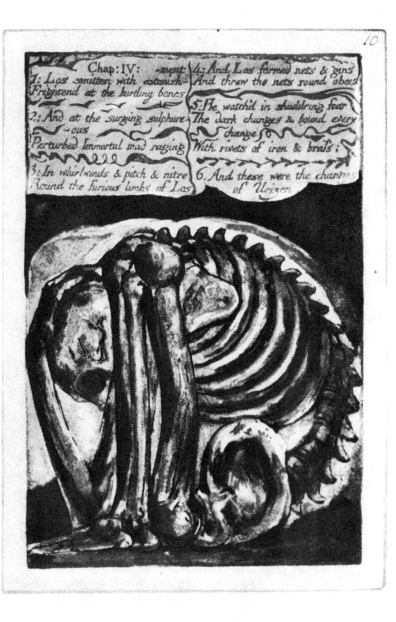

Chap: IV.

1 Ages on ages rolld over him!       Settled, a lake, bright, & shining clear
In stony sleep ages rolld over him!   White as the snow on the mountains cold.
Like a dark waste stretching chang'able
By earthquakes riv'n, belching sullen   4 Forgetfulness, dumbness, necessity!
    fires                              In chains of the mind locked up,
On ages rolld ages in ghastly         Like fetters of ice shrinking together
Sick torment; around him in whirlwinds  Disorganiz'd, rent from Eternity.
Of darkness the eternal Prophet howl'd  Los beat on his fetters of iron.
Beating still on his rivets of iron   And heated his furnaces & pour'd
Pouring sodor of iron; dividing       Iron sodor and sodor of brass
The horrible night into watches.
                                      5 Restless turnd the immortal inchain'd
2 And Urizen (so his eternal name)    Heaving dolorous, anguish'd, unbearable
His prolific delight obscurd more & more  Till a roof shaggy wild inclos'd
In dark secresy hiding in surgeing    In an orb, his fountain of thought.
Sulphureous fluid his phantasies.
The Eternal Prophet heavd the dark    6 In a horrible dreamful slumber;
    bellows,                          Like the linked infernal chain;
And turnd restless the tongs; and the   A vast Spine writh'd in torment
    hammer                            Upon the winds; shooting pain'd
Incessant beat; forging chains new & new  Ribs, like a bending cavern
Numb'ring with links, hours, days & years  And bones of solidness, froze
                                      Over all his nerves of joy.
3 The eternal mind bounded began to roll  And a first Age passed over,
Eddies of wrath ceasless round & round  And a state of dismal woe.
And the sulphureous foam surgeing thick

7 From the caverns of his jointed Spine
Down sunk with fright a red
Round globe hot burning deep
Deep down into the Abyss:
Panting: Conglobing; Trembling
Shooting out ten thousand branches
Around his solid bones,
And a second Age passed over,
And a state of dismal woe.

In harrowing fear rolled round:
But no more breath still branching
From the branches of his heart
Like into two little orbs
.... in two little caves

Hissing carefully from the ....
His Eyes beheld the ....
And a third Age passed over,
And a state of dismal woe.

9 The pangs of hope began,
In heavy pain striving, striving,
Two Ears in close volutions
From beneath his orbs of vision
Shot spiring out and petrified
As they grew from the deep pit
And a state of dismal woe.

10 In ghastly torment sick,
Hanging upon the ....
....

## 15

Urizen C: V.

His Nostrils bent down to the deep. | In trembling & howling & dismay.
And a Fifth Age passed over; | And a seventh Age pulsed over:
And a state of dismal woe. | And a state of dismal woe.

11. In ghastly torment sick; | Chap: V.
Within his ribs bloated round. |
A craving Hungry Cavern; | 1. In terrors Los shrunk from his
Thence arose his channeld Throat | task:
And like a red flame a Tongue | His great hammer fell from his hand.
Of thirst & of hunger appeard | His fires beheld, and sickening.
And a sixth Age passed over: | Hid their strong limbs in smoke.
And a state of dismal woe. | For with noises ruinous loud;
| With hurtlings & clashings & groans
12. Enraged & stifled with torment | The Immortal endur'd his chains,
He threw his right Arm to the north | Tho' bound in a deadly sleep.
His left Arm to the south |
Shooting out in anguish deep. | 2. All the myriads of Eternity;
And his Feet stampd the nether Abyss | All the wisdom & joy of life:
| Roll like a sea around him,

Except what his little orbs | Then he look'd back with anxious desire
Of sight by degrees unfold. | But the space undivided by existence
| Struck horror into his soul.
3. And now his eternal life |
Like a dream was obliterated | 6. Los wept obscur'd with mourning:
| His bosom earthquak'd with sighs;
4. Shuddring, the Eternal Prophet smote | He saw Urizen deadly black,
With a stroke, from his north to south | In his chains bound, & Pity began.
region |
The bellows & hammer are silent now | 7. In anguish dividing & dividing
A nerveless silence, his prophetic voice | For pity divides the soul
Siez'd; a cold solitude & dark void | In pangs eternity on eternity
The Eternal Prophet & Urizen closd | Life in cataracts pourd down his
| cliffs
5. Ages on ages rolld over them | The void shrunk the lymph into Nerves
Cut off from life & light frozen | Wandring wide on the bosom of night
Into horrible forms of deformity | And left a round globe of blood
Los suffer'd his fires to decay | Trembling upon the Void

## 16

Thus the Eternal Prophet was divided    At the dark separation appeard
Before the dark image of Urizen      As glasses discover Worlds
For in changeable clouds and darkness   In the endless Abyss of space,
In a horrible night beneath        So the expanding eyes of Immortals
The Abyss of Los stretch'd immense:   Beheld the dark visions of Los,
And now seen now obscurd to the eyes   And the globe of life blood trembling
Of Eternals, the visions remote

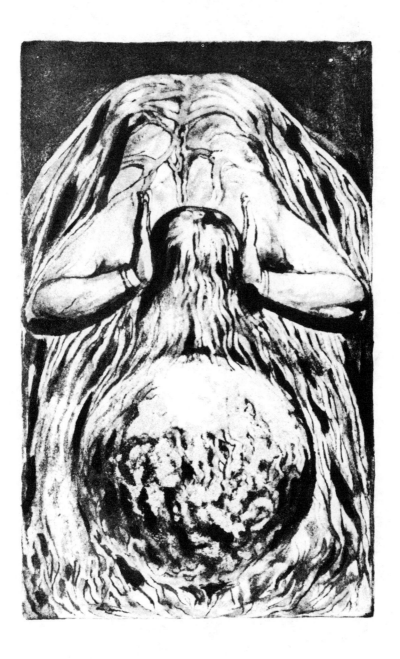

Urizen C: V.

8. The globe of life blood trembled
Branching out into roots:
Fibrous, writhing upon the winds:
Fibres of blood, milk and tears:
In pangs, eternity on eternity
At length in tears & cries imbodied
A female form trembling and pale
Waves before his deathy face

9. All Eternity shudderd at sight
Of the first female now separate
Pale as a cloud of snow
Waving before the face of Los

10. Wonder, awe, fear, astonishment
Petrify the eternal myriads;
At the first female form now separate

They call'd her Pity, and fled

11. Spread a Tent, with strong cur-
  tains around them
"Let cords & stakes bind in the Void
That Eternals may no more behold them"

12. They began to weave curtains of
  darkness
They erected large pillars round the Void
With golden hooks fasten'd in the pillars
With infinite labour the Eternals
A woof wove, and called it Science.

   Chap: VI

1. But Los saw the Female & pitied
He embrac'd her, she wept, she refus'd
In perverse and cruel delight
She fled from his arms, yet he follow'd

2. Eternity shudder'd when they saw
Man begetting his likeness
On his own divided image.

3. A time passed over, the Eternals
Began to erect the tent;
When Enitharmon sick,
Felt a Worm within her womb.

4. Yet helpless it lay like a Worm
In the trembling womb
To be moulded into existence

5. All day the worm lay on her bosom
All night within her womb
The worm lay till it grew to a ser-
  pent
With dolorous hissings & poisons
Round Enitharmons loins folding.

6. Coild within Enitharmons womb
The serpent grew casting its scales
With sharp pangs the hissings began
To change to a grating cry,
Many sorrows and dismal throes,
Many forms of fish, bird & beast,
Brought forth an Infant form
Where was a worm before.

7. The Eternals their tent finished
Alarm'd with these gloomy visions
When Enitharmon groaning
Produc'd a man Child to the light.

8. A shriek ran thro' Eternity:
And a paralytic stroke;
At the birth of the Human shadow.

9. Delving earth in his resistless
  way;
Howling, the Child with fierce flames
Issued from Enitharmon.

10. The Eternals, closed the tent
They beat down the stakes the cords

Urizen C: VII

Stretch'd for a work of eternity:
No more Los beheld Eternity.

11. In his hands he siezd the infant
He bathed him in springs of sorrow
He gave him to Enitharmon.

Chap. VII

1. They named the child Orc, he grew
Fed with milk of Enitharmon.

2. Los awoke her, O sorrow & pain.
A tightening girdle grew
Around his bosom. In sobbings
He burst the girdle in twain.
But still another girdle
Opressd his bosom. In sobbings
Again he burst it Again
Another girdle succeeds
The girdle was formd by day:
By night was burst in twain.

3. These falling down on the rock
Into an iron Chain
In each other link by link lockd

4. They took Orc to the top of a
        mountain.
O how Enitharmon wept!
They chaind his young limbs to the
        rock
With the Chain of Jealousy
Beneath Urizens deathful shadow

5. The dead heard the voice of the
        child
And began to awake from sleep
All things, heard the voice of the child
And began to awake to life.

6. And Urizen craving with hunger
Stung with the odours of Nature
Explord his dens around

7. He formd a line & a plummet
To divide the Abyss beneath.
He formd a dividing rule:

8. He formd scales to weigh:
He formed massy weights.
He formed a brazen quadrant.
He formed golden compasses
And began to explore the Abyss
And he planted a garden of fruits

9. But Los encircled Enitharmon
With fires of Prophecy
From the sight of Urizen & Orc.

10. And she bore an enormous race

Chap. VIII.

1. Urizen explord his dens
Mountain, moor, & wilderness,
With a globe of fire lighting his
        journey
A fearful journey, annoy'd
By cruel enormities: forms

Urizen Ch VIII

Of life on his forsaken mountains

2. And his world teemd vast enormities
Frightning; faithless; yawning
Portions of life; similitudes
Of a foot, or a hand, or a head
Or a heart, or an eye, they swam mis
  -chevous
Dread terrors! delighting in blood

3. Most Urizen sickend to see
His eternal creations appear
Sons & daughters of sorrow on mountains
Weeping! wailing! first Thiriel appeard
Astonishd at his own existance
Like a man from a cloud born, & Utha
From the waters emerging laments!

Grodna rent the deep earth howling
Amazd! his heavens immense cracks
Like the ground parchd with heat; then
Fuzon
Flam'd out! first begotten, last born.
All his eternal sons in like manner
His daughters from green herbs & cattle
From monsters, & worms of the pit.

4. He in darkness closd, view'd all his
  race
And his soul sickend! he cursd
Both sons & daughters; for he saw
That no flesh nor spirit could keep
His iron laws one moment.

5. For he saw that life livd upon
  death

The Ox in the slaughter house moans
The Dog at the wintry door
And he wept, & he called it Pity
And his tears flowed down on the winds

6. Cold he wanderd on high, over
their cities
In weeping & pain & woe!
And wherever he wanderd in sorrows
Upon the aged heavens
A cold shadow follow'd behind him
Like a spiders web, moist, cold, & dim
Drawing out from his sorrowing soul
The dungeon-like heaven dividing
Where-ever the footsteps of Urizen
Walkd over the cities in sorrow.

7. Till a Web dark & cold, throughout all
The tormented element stretch'd
From the sorrows of Urizens soul
And the Web is a Female in embrio
None could break the Web, no wings
of fire

8. So twisted the cords, & so knotted
The meshes: twisted like to the
human brain

9. And all calld it, The Net of Reli-

Chap: IX

1. Then the Inhabitants of those Cities;
Felt their Nerves change into Marrow
And hardening Bones began
In swift diseases and torments,
In throbbings & shootings & grindings
Thro all the coasts; till weakend
The Senses inward rush'd shrinking,
Beneath the dark net of infection.

2. Till the shrunken eyes clouded over
Discernd not the woven hipocrisy
But the streaky slime in their heavens
Brought together by narrowing perceptions
Appeard transparent air; for their eyes
Grew small like the eyes of a man
And in reptile forms shrinking together
Of seven feet stature they remaind

3. Six days they shrunk up from existence
And on the seventh day they rested
And they blessd the seventh day, in sick
hope:
And forgot their eternal life

4. And their thirty cities divided
In form of a human heart
No more could they rise at will
In the infinite void, but bound down
To earth by their narrowing perceptions

Urizen. C:IX.

They lived a period of years
Then left a noisom body
To the jaws of devouring darkness

For the ears of the inhabitants,
Were wither'd, & deafend, & cold:
And their eyes could not discern,
Their brethren of other cities.

5. And their children wept, & built
Tombs in the desolate places,
And form'd laws of prudence, and
           call'd them
The eternal laws of God

8. So Fuzon call'd all together
The remaining children of Urizen:
And they left the pendulous earth:
They called it Egypt, & left it.

6. And the thirty cities remaind
Surround'd by salt floods, now call'd
Africa: its name was then Egypt.

9. And the salt ocean rolled englob'd

7. The remaining sons of Urizen
Beheld their brethren shrink together
Beneath the Net of Urizen:
Perswasion was in vain

The End of the
book of Urizen